Praise for Si§

"Gives good advice on improving your game."
— Bruno Alvarez, Indirect Spend Manager, Guatemala

"★★★★★ Another inspirational read from Sigi! Full of useful tips on how to progress within your career and make the most of opportunities."
— Amazon Customer

"Your book is a delightful read! … with sensible and realistic guidance which I'm already applying."
— Susan M., Baltimore, USA

"Sigi has been a fantastic coach and mentor to me … he helped me sail through a couple of job promotions. A truly great coach and mentor."
— HG, Regional Manager, Financial Services, UK

"His content is powerful, concise and invaluable … will have a long-lasting, immensely positive effect upon the Burberry team."
— Stuart Pemble, Group CPO, Burberry

"★★★★★ Super brilliant! Full of priceless advice; some of it makes you really stop and think … And quite inspiring … 'Highly recommend it."

— Barnes & Noble Customer

"A practical guide, based on experience … thoroughly engaging … refreshingly inspirational."

— *Engineering & Technology*

"Sigi coached our team to improve our effectiveness … he helped me sharpen my own professional capabilities … a brilliant coach and mentor."

— Ben Wilmot, Program Manager, Ericsson AB

"Very readable and enjoyable … many useful tips and tricks … his advice is well worth taking."

— *Spend Matters*

"★★★★★ This book allows you to look at yourself and helps you make life-changing decisions which will allow you to reach your full potential."

— Amazon Customer

"Everyone should have a Sigi in their cupboard!"

— Sonia Fatkin, Oxfordshire, UK

ALSO BY SIGI OSAGIE

Sweet Stakeholder Love: Powerful Insights and Tactics to Deal with Stakeholder Issues Better and Achieve More Success at Work

Procurement Mojo®: Strengthening the Function and Raising Its Profile

25 Quotes & 75 Questions to Boost Your Thinking on Procurement Success

*

Available at: SigiOsagie.com

REVISED AND EXPANDED EDITION

Career Dreams
to
Career Success

CONVERSATIONS WITH A MENTOR

SIGI OSAGIE

❤

First published in e-book only © 2018.
This edition published in 2023 by EPG Solutions Limited
Registered Office: The Old Bakery, Blackborough Road, Reigate, Surrey
RH2 7BU, United Kingdom
www.sigiosagie.com

Copyright © EPG Solutions Limited 2023

Contains extracts from other works by Sigi Osagie © 2006–2022

Sigi Osagie asserts the moral right to be identified as the author of this work

Editing by Karen Morton Editorial Services
Cover design by Tanja Prokop and interior design,
formatting & typesetting by Graciela Aničić (Bookcoverworld.com)
Bottles image in Passion article tweet by Jalyn Bryce via Pixabay

ISBN (paperback): 978-1-8384892-2-9
ISBN (e-book): 978-1-8384892-3-6

To my mum and dad, Victoria and Tony,
who gave me the best foundation upon which to build
my career success.
Thank you both for everything.

Contents

Author's Note

EVERYBODY WANTS SUCCESS. BUT NOT everybody knows how to get it. Kudos to you for getting this book to learn the strategies that will help you achieve the career success you want.

The very fact that you are here right now reading these words says something about you; that something will be a critical factor in materializing your success.

My own desire for success is what set me on the path to expanding my learning many years ago. It was the same learning that elevated me from a near barefoot and penniless immigrant, through a tremendously successful and fulfilling corporate career, to writing these words presently. Now I share what I've learned in this book.

You will gain the knowledge of the most crucial things you need to flourish and excel, and invaluable guidance to steer your career ship shrewdly and achieve your desired success.

It's much the same guidance I provide to my coaching and mentoring clients. Their subsequent successes and feedback often indicate to me how fruitful my advice is. And it's those outcomes that inspired me to provide these salient points as a compact package, which is the book you're reading now. So you too can accomplish similar triumphs in your career.

Some of the guidance here is presented as articles, anecdotes and analogies. Some as bite-sized nuggets of wisdom to chew on and act on. And others as explicit tips and extracts of my social media posts. They all distill powerful insights and tactics that will help you thrive and succeed in your career.

Keep an open mind as you read. Don't discount any of the principles or tips until you've digested them fully and tried them out. The ingredients of career success may not be what conventional wisdom has led you to believe, and this isn't a conventional career advice book. Conventional wisdom typically yields conventional results, i.e., standard, normal, ordinary. The success you want is not ordinary—if it was, *everybody* would achieve it. The career success that awaits you is extraordinary.

Success is always preceded by the dream of success. Just as your route to career success starts with your career dreams.

Career Dreams: Your Chariot to the Gods

THE VIEW FROM MY OFFICE window offered such a splendid panoramic vista it made me envy myself. I couldn't help the happy smile that lingered on my face as I soaked in the breathtaking scenery.

The lush, rolling hillsides were like endless waves of vibrant green, juxtaposed with patches of straw-yellow and earthy light-brown hues that marked out the farm fields. A picturesque canvas that was made more enchanting by the beautiful río Guadalquivir in the distance. The rays of the golden sun kissed the river in places, and it glistened as if in response as it snaked its way through the landscape.

Even the great Picasso could never have done justice to this scene.

Having my desk up here, right at the top of the tower of my Spanish castle, was like sitting on the roof of the world. It made me feel close to the gods in the sky. What a magnificent location to do my work.

Brrring, brrring. Brrring, brrring ... The sudden, insistent buzzing of my phone jolted me back to earth from my castle in the sky.

I picked up the phone thinking to myself, "Wouldn't it be great if the gods permitted me to use my voodoo magic powers to get my office-atop-the-castle just by dreaming of it?"

But even as I thought it, I already knew what the gods would say: that *action* is always essential to achieve my career goals.

No matter how modest or lofty one's ambitions are, you've got to take intentional action to achieve what you want. That means not waiting for things to happen but making them happen.

But whenever I think of my own lofty goals, I can't help getting lost in a dream—a dream of savoring the sweet nectar of success.

I once spent a couple of years dreaming of living in the UK, at a time when I barely had two cents to my name, in a far-off land somewhere in Africa where I walked about with big, gaping holes in my shoes.

And then one day, I woke up from my dream and found myself stepping off a plane at London's Heathrow Airport!

Soon afterwards, I spent a fair bit of time dreaming of finding a job, so I could earn money to send back to Africa so my five wives could have ample supplies of cows, goats and chickens.

And then, despite arriving in the UK in the middle of what I later learned was a "recession," I found two jobs!

A few years on, I was dreaming of having a successful corporate career, rather than earning my living by washing dishes, mopping floors and cleaning toilets.

And lo and behold, I awoke from my dream to find that I was a global director with responsibilities spanning thirteen or so countries in a blue-chip FTSE 250 conglomerate!

I suspect that I may be addicted to dreaming.

But I've discovered that I'm not the only one who dreams; apparently, many successful people in all walks of life do too. They dream about the accomplishments they become famous for—but we rarely hear or know of the dreams, just the ensuing success that manifests in reality. We know more of Bill Gates's success than his early dreams about a computer on every office desk and in every home. Likewise, we know more of *Harry Potter* than J.K. Rowling's dreams of becoming a writer. And it's the same with George Lucas and *Star Wars*; Sylvester Stallone and *Rocky*; and Howard Schultz and Starbucks.

It seems like I could be onto something with my addiction. Perhaps my dreams have also become addicted—they seem to have formed a habit of manifesting into reality.

So I'll keep dreaming.

But I also keep checking with myself, by asking:

❖ Is the work you're doing now what you dreamed you'd be doing this time last year?

❖ Or is the work you're doing now a stepping stone that gets you closer to the realization of your career dreams?

❖ Or is the work you're doing now exactly just that: "work"—work that doesn't fulfill your spirit and is simply dancing to someone else's drumbeat in return for dollars?

And the answers seem to have a modulating effect on my subsequent dreams and actions. *Ay, caramba!*

I sense that my dreams are like chariots to the gods, sending forth my heartfelt desires, because the gods have no cell phones or emails. And when those desires are congruent with my authentic self, the gods give their acknowledgment. But I only find out their decision by trying to reach my dreams here on earth.

My dreams always seem to steer me in indescribable ways toward my career goals, like the currents of the ocean that can guide a lost ship to a safe haven.

But trusting the guidance of my dreams is no easy accomplishment.

My dreams can be a hard taskmaster, pushing me to do what needs doing rather than waiting until *mañana*. At those times, I feel the pull of their potent effect like a voodoo spell that pervades my being until I'm compelled to "get on with it." Sometimes, that means work—the heavy labor that is required to build castles on the ground, including some tasks I may not enjoy. Other times, it means a good sleep, rest, play or laughter—to give myself a break from the toil, so I can emerge from the respite with recharged vitality. And sometimes, it's simply about finding the silence of solitude—to fade out the voices of the outer world, sit still and tune into the song of my inner voice, so I can sing it with verve and gusto.

Whatever it means, it's always about using the moment. Because the present moment is what separates the past from the future; each moment of life is a gap between what went before and what is to come. So the past and the future are interlinked by our thoughts, feelings and actions in the moment.

It's as if my dreams whisper softly to my spirit: "Sigi, it's exactly 11:11 a.m. on Wednesday January 11, 2023. You will never get this moment again. So use it wisely, to weave the tapestry of the future you desire."

At times like this, I can't argue with the wisdom of my dreams.

Yet my dreams can also be a tormentor, bringing me sorrow and anguish; at those times when my impatience gets the better of me or I'm overwhelmed by so many things not going to plan. My desires remain so strong yet the frustrations can be disheartening. That's when I'm moved to tears. And I let myself cry.

I let myself cry because it's part of being human, voo-doo magician or not. I cry because something somewhere deep inside of me knows that the tears that fall from my eyes are like the droplets of water that make up the ocean. The same ocean whose currents can guide lost ships, the way my dreams guide me on the voyage of career success.

When things click into place and I'm in my groove, I can feel the flow of the currents of my dreams in my work. It's like a rhythm that inspires my spirit and inflames my passion, evoking a mysterious, magical fire that consumes every aspect of my psyche, much like *el duende* that pos-sesses the ardent flamenco dancers of Andalucía.

And whenever those currents steer me to my desti-nation port—like touching down at Heathrow Airport, getting my first kitchen porter job or reading the organ-ization announcement that proclaimed my appointment as a global director just fourteen years later—I'm moved to tears yet again. And as if on cue, I hear the whisper of my dreams once more.

They remind me that my tears of sorrow have become tears of joy. And that the prize always exceeds the price.

They tell me so many other things, things that are really ineffable, things that mirror the ecstasy of that moment when dream becomes reality.

You know what I'm talking about, because you've been there before. Haven't you? You've heard that whisper in the moment of victory several times.

I heard it when I got my first consultancy assignment, having taken a leap of faith off the corporate hamster wheel. I heard it too when I secured my first speaking engagement. And I heard it when I signed up my first coaching and mentoring client; the first time my writing appeared in a trade magazine; and the day my first book was published.

I have a feeling I'll be hearing that whisper yet again pretty soon.

Do you have that same feeling—the sense, hunch or notion, that unexplainable inner knowing that you're close to the moment when your dream meets reality?

Experience has taught me that there can be lots of hard slog between the dream and the manifested reality; because dreams don't build castles and castles don't build themselves.

And I've learned that there are several ingredients that go into weaving the tapestry of that reality; too many to list here, but they certainly include:

❖ The self-leadership to steer through the ups and downs of the career adventure

❖ The courage to face the inevitable doubts and fears that arise

❖ The self-discipline to spend my time on things that propel me toward my career goals

❖ The wisdom to invest money in my career development

❖ The intelligence to seek out people whose experiences I can learn from

❖ The determination to fight for my dreams, because I refuse to take them to my grave with me

❖ The good sense to choose *mis compañeros* with care and immerse myself in environments that are conducive to my flourishing

❖ The patience to let the fruit ripen in its own perfect time, because it forces me to slow down and synchronize my pace with the clock of life, and a patient person will always eat ripe fruit

❖ The flexibility to recognize when life is giving me a better scheme of stepping stones, especially when they're disguised as challenges

❖ The good luck that often shows up as "preparation" meeting "opportunity"

❖ The humility to never think that my job title, my Savile Row suits or my dollars in the bank make me more important than the cleaning lady, because I too was once a cleaner

❖ The self-belief that comes from knowing that life has faith in me, just as it has faith in you; so I must have faith in life, in myself and in my ability to achieve my career dreams.

My dreams are always waiting for me; I hear their call in the depths of my heart—they tell me that they want to manifest into reality just as much as I want them to.

So, yes, I will keep dreaming. Dreaming of doing work that fills me with enthusiasm. And dreaming of singing my song to make my heart smile in ecstasy.

And so should you. Because, just like mine, your career dreams are your chariot to the gods of success.

But what do you dream of? And what do your dreams tell you when you hear their call?

Nuggets for Your Success

***

If you have no dreams, then what?

***

***

Dreams don't build castles and castles don't build themselves. But it's the dream of the castle that inspires and spurs you to start building.

What's your career dream, and what does your "castle" look like in your dream?

***

***

"Nobody can make you give up on your dreams;
only you."
— @SigiOsagie

***

Sigi Osagie

Writer, Speaker, Business Adviser & Coach + Mentor. Author, SWEET STAKEHOLDER LOVE

3y

Is the #work you're doing right now, today, this week or this month fulfilling your spirit? Or are you simply dancing to someone else's drumbeat in return for dollars?

Every one of us is filled with the hungry spirit of human potential that thirsts for fulfilment. A big part of fulfilment is doing work that brings out the best in us, helps us grow and feeds our hungry spirit.

19

***

"Deep down inside, many of us would like to do more and be more in our lives. But most people don't, for a variety of reasons.

Will YOU be inspired to triumph and create your own legend?"

— @SigiOsagie

***

***

"I'm not a neuroscientist, just a plain old voodoo priest. But I've always believed in the power of humor and laughter in the #workplace. I have no scientific 'proof' other than personal experience.

Oftentimes at #work, we take things too seriously and forget that we are all still humans, with beating hearts within us.

If you have a beating heart inside you, every beat of that heart is a gentle cue reminding you of the potential within you and your obligation to unleash your immeasurable capabilities. And every beat is also a reminder of your humanity. Humor is a powerful attribute of the human soul, a bequest from the gods which we receive at birth. It's one of the richest and freshest ingredients in the alchemy of a healthy life; and a healthy life produces auspicious outcomes.

So try to laugh at work at least once today—and every day. Your heart will be smiling when you do that, and it's more likely to sing its song when it smiles ☺

May your life be filled with copious smiles and laughter."

— Linkedin.com/in/SigiOsagie

***

***

"What would your #worklife look like if you measured every decision you made against your #career goals/aspirations?"
— @SigiOsagie

***

***

"Seeing is believing."

Yet believing can also result in seeing.

And some of the most important things in life cannot be seen. Like the air we breathe that keeps us alive; the thoughts, emotions and impulses we experience that often drive our actions, and hence shape our lives; and the thing we feel inside when we snuggle up to our loved ones.

Many of those most important things abound in our work life, if we pay adequate attention. And they often lead us to discovering and harnessing our best selves.

*

"Seeing is believing."

Yet you can create another believable world if you close your eyes and stop seeing, a world replete with oceans of possibilities.

One of those possibilities is this: What if, just what if, you really can achieve your career dreams?

*

"Seeing is believing."

Yet believing can also result in seeing.

You'll start seeing your success when you *truly* believe it; and act accordingly.

***

***

Be clear and know what you desire. Leverage the power of your thoughts and imagination by visualizing your goals frequently; it's good for your mojo.

Imagine yourself achieving the success or outcomes you want—*see yourself there, and feel what it'll feel like when you're there*; experience the experience of your success in your mind's eye, and let yourself bask in it fully in your imagination without any limitations.

Feed your psyche with this vivid dream regularly. And accompany your vision with related actions.

***

***

"Fortune certainly smiles on those who are brave enough
to pursue their destiny. Are you?"
— @SigiOsagie

***

Sigi Osagie
@SigiOsagie

Life has faith in you. So you must have faith in yourself and your ability to achieve your #career dreams.

> **Life has faith in you
> — that's why you're
> <u>alive</u>.
> Do you have faith in life?**
>
>
> sigiOSAGIE
> Delivers Effectiveness & Performance Growth
>
> © Sigi Osagie, 2017
> www.sigiosagie.com

The Mountain Climber

REACHING FOR YOUR CAREER DREAMS can be a very rewarding and fulfilling experience, filled with many moments of joy. But the journey can also be fraught with disappointments, frustrations, fear and pain.

However, it's the kind of sweet pain a mountain climber feels in her aching muscles as she makes one step after another toward the summit.

Even when the mountaintop seems so distant, she continues with the endeavor, one step after another, one step after another, one step after another … The rhythm of the sweet pain keeps the tempo of her endeavor and reminds her of the dream in her heart: to reach the mountaintop.

She knows that every ache she feels means she's a step closer, and she must bear the aches to reach the top. Just as the metal bears the blows of the blacksmith's hammer to become a valuable tool. Just as the land bears the dark night to see the glory of the next sunrise. Just as the tree bears the loss of its leaves to survive the cycle and thrive in the coming seasons.

It's all part of the experience, the experience of her coming victory.

And there is no shortcut to victory. Those who claim to have a formula for racing swiftly to the top of Everest are charlatans and false prophets, no better than the multitude of snake-oil salesmen the internet has bred who peddle various "hacks" as shortcuts to overnight success.

She knows she must take her time and not rush the process. In fact, she can't; the process is what it is. You can't make the tree grow faster. The caterpillar can't morph into a butterfly quicker. And the clouds can't turn into rainfall swifter.

She has heard many tales of other climbers who didn't respect the process and tried to circumvent it. The process rewarded their haste by asking the mountain to teach them valuable lessons. Some ended up missing their step in their hurry and fell to their death. Others lost their traction and suffered sprained ankles or severe injuries; some even lost their limbs.

She doesn't want a Pyrrhic victory. So rather than trying to hurry, she focuses her attention on the evolving process of her ascent, matching her footsteps and her gait to the lay of the land, so she doesn't lose her balance. She knows her ultimate success will come from choosing her steps with due consideration, and making each step itself an individual success.

Her body still aches. Her spirit is somewhat weary. And her mind is like an untrained monkey, jumping from one thought to another like from tree branch to tree branch.

Sometimes it's preoccupied with thoughts of inspiration at the prospect of reaching the summit. And that fills her with enthusiasm. She likes that; because she remembers that the original meaning of the root word—*enthous*—is to be possessed by a god. So anything which fills her with enthusiasm is good for her soul.

At other times her mind is filled with uncertainty, trepidation and thoughts of failure, saying to her, "You can't achieve this … Why don't you just stick with the safe and comfortable … What if you don't succeed …"

She knows her mind has her best interests at heart. But she also knows that if she doesn't control it, her mind will end up controlling her.

And she must control it, and protect it too—it's a precious real estate where her success is built before taking form in the real world. If she doesn't protect it, it could become overrun with psychological vermin, like fear, doubt and worry; unwelcome visitors who could easily become permanent squatters.

She knows her mind is awaiting her response or reaction; it probably expects her obedience, because it sometimes thinks it is her lord and master and it knows it all.

But her mind cannot understand everything that happens in life, especially the affairs of climbing mountains. There are some issues of the climb that exceed the logical capacities of her rational mind, things that her second brain, which resides in her gut, can often sense.

She chooses her words carefully, because she knows that words have power. She also knows that whatever she says to her mind she's saying to herself. And her self-talk is potent.

She replies to her mind, "Well, we've come this far, let's see how much further we can go; perhaps it may be all the way to the top, which is what I truly desire. Besides, I believe in the depths of my soul that this is what I was born to do, like the bird was born to fly and the fish to swim. I'll only know for sure by trying. So dear wonderful mind of mine, you amazing and powerful tool that helps me in so many ways, please stop worrying about problems that haven't occurred and may never occur, and let's keep going."

Her will to win pushes her on. Her grit gives her stamina. And she makes each successive step with determination, trusting that the process will impart its wisdom to her, through the conduit of her focus and dedication. It's the wisdom that she'll use to create reality from the seeds of her dream.

She has dreamed the dream many times before, visualizing herself at the mountaintop and delighting in the feeling of what it'd be like to be up there.

And each time she dreamed, the dream became more vivid. So her goal is clear in her mind.

She has prepared soundly for her climb and planned her route, making necessary adjustments to her plan along the way to allow for the reality of the mountain terrain.

Because she's attuned to the prospects and pitfalls on her path and she's true to herself, she knows that providence will smile upon her efforts.

Dwelling on the dream itself no longer matters; it's the actions she's taking right now that count. So she concentrates on each individual step as she takes it, despite the dream that remains in her heart, the dream that won't die, that engulfs her and keeps her going, ever closer to the mountaintop with each step she takes. A mountain climber.

Those who really want more out of their careers, who refuse to compromise and want to reach for the best within themselves, are mountain climbers—because the journey to career success (however you define success) often entails a series of mountains: challenges which stretch us *and teach us* as we attempt to overcome them.

Some people wake up in the morning, look up to the top of the mountain, ponder for a bit, and then say, "Tomorrow …"

Others wake up and try to avoid gazing at the mountaintop—they prefer to pretend the mountain isn't there.

Mountain climbers relish the challenge of pushing themselves beyond what seems possible, knowing that every ache they bear will help them to become more valuable, to enjoy many glorious sunrises, and to thrive through many seasons. They know that as difficult as the climb may be, it also helps them build muscle.

That's what makes the pain sweet: the inner knowledge that despite the disappointments, frustrations, fears and aches, with every step of the journey you're closer to reaching your career dreams.

So don't stop. Your dreams are waiting for you.

Passion Is a Requisite Elixir

I SMILED TO MYSELF AS I admired the rhythmic flow of her gait, and how she carried herself with the elegance that is so characteristic of many French women. As she ambled along the Promenade des Anglais she exuded that indescribable vibe that comes from being comfortable in your own skin, a certain *je ne sais quoi*.

I caught myself in my reverie, and remembered that this experience of watching the world go by, lost in the beauty of each moment and appreciating the special energy of the Côte d'Azur, is why I love the city of Nice.

I'm here on my customary retreat to revamp my own energies and nourish my mojo. I've found this habit of taking time out to check under the hood periodically to be invaluable. And I try to do this at least once a year—not a holiday, just time to "be" and tune into my soul.

I shouldn't be "working," yet the fact that I'm writing this proves otherwise. But I'm writing this piece right now because I'm driven by passion. And I can tell you, this doesn't feel like "work" in any way!

I like to go with the flow at such times, because I know that my passion is the fuel that sustains me on my adventure to nurture my best self. So I listen when it speaks.

And I don't have to come to Nice in particular for that to happen. It happens in many other places too, because passion isn't a French thing; it's a universal language we all understand.

You know how it feels when you're doing things with passion—sadly, some of us only feel that vibe with our hobbies and rarely bring it to the workplace; or it gets snuffed out by inept bosses and toxic organizational cultures. But when we do, work never seems like "work." And that's when we often discover or reveal our true capabilities and do some of our best work.

People with passion bring energy to organizations. That's why esteemed business leaders treasure this characteristic in people. Steve Jobs, the late Apple boss, believed people with passion can change the world. And Jack Welch, ex-Chairman and CEO of GE, who was once named "Manager of the Century" by *Fortune* magazine, described it as a "powerfully game-changing quality."

Do you feel the power of your passion in the work you're doing?

If not, you should ask yourself why.

And don't wait for things to change; change things yourself—'could be your perspectives, your thought processes, your attitude to the job, or maybe even changing jobs and moving to something that gets your juices flowing.

And if you manage people, you must think about whether or not you're igniting and harnessing their passion to aid their success and yours.

Success at work and in your career is multifaceted, irrespective of your professional field. There are hard, technical aspects like workplace processes, technology, and so on. And there are soft elements too; like relationships, self-leadership and passion—the intangible factors that are often the underlying differentiators between success stories and tales of woe.

Passion alone doesn't bring success, but it's a requisite elixir to get yourself firing on all cylinders.

It's nigh on impossible to do your work with heart and operate at peak performance if you have no passion for your work.

Nigella Lawson isn't a great chef just by luck; neither is Lionel Messi a prodigious soccer player nor Warren

Buffett a successful business magnate simply by accident. They have a passion for their game, just like that other consummate chef, Gordon Ramsay.

The key ingredient in the wonderful meals Ramsay creates is his miscellany of culinary skills—skills that are honed every time he steps into a kitchen. But he only goes in there because he has a passion for his game.

Do you have a passion for yours?

Nuggets for Your Success

***

"You learned that if you play with fire you'll get burned, from your parent(s) at home.

You learned that if you add two and two you get four, from your teacher at school.

You learned that if you stand in the rain you'll get wet, from nature out there.

But where did you learn that you can't or won't achieve your #career dreams?"

— Linkedin.com/in/SigiOsagie

***

***

"We're making choices every day that shape our life story and our career destiny. As you face up to your choices with your goals and aspirations:

- ❖ Will you say 'Tomorrow …'?
- ❖ Or will you 'pretend the mountain isn't there'?
- ❖ Or will you be a mountain climber?

Whatever choice you make, the clock of life is always ticking."

— @SigiOsagie

***

***

If you keep facing the same issues or challenges in different situations in your career, then maybe you should stop and reflect: is life trying to tell you something? Perhaps there are one or two things you need to learn from these repeated experiences.

Reflecting on your past, your desired future and your current dispositions, without getting trapped in any negative emotions or pessimistic thoughts, helps expand your wisdom and your intimacy with yourself and your dreams.

***

***

Your passion is the fire that will sustain you on your career journey.

Passion is the critical fuel that keeps us invigorated, especially in challenging times or when things aren't quite going to plan—your passion will be a key aid that will help you in overcoming challenges in your work and impel you toward your métier.

***

***

When our passions are ignited and our juices are flowing, we're in tune with our mojos; and motivation and inspiration are much easier.

And when we work with motivation and inspiration, we create miracles and magic, we excel at what we do.

When you have passion for what you do, self-belief comes more naturally, and growth is easier because you enjoy what you do.

***

***

You're more likely to find your groove, thrive and excel if you make your career choices based on passion.

❖ What makes you come alive?
❖ What gets your juices flowing?

***

***

Think of your favorite actor, sportsperson, musician, business leader, etc. Perhaps it may be one of these famous top performers:

Adele; Oprah Winfrey; Eric Clapton; Lewis Hamilton; Cristiano Ronaldo; Richard Branson; Serena Williams; J.K. Rowling; Jennifer Lawrence; Bill Gates; Barbra Streisand; Isabel Allende; Denzel Washington; Michael Jordan; …

Do you think these people are/were successful in their careers by sheer luck, or because they just happen to be good at their thing, … or because their passion for their thing keeps/kept them spending time and effort at it, hence honing their abilities all the time and feeding their spirit?

What do you think?

***

Sigi Osagie
@SigiOsagie

"Your passion is the fuel that will sustain you when your career adventure gets rocky. So listen when it speaks.":

sigiosagie.com
Passion Is a Requisite Elixir –
Sigi Osagie

***

"Challenges in life or at #work are somewhat like mountains.

Mountains exist to be viewed, contemplated, and so we can enjoy their magnificence. And perhaps mountains exist also to be climbed and conquered.

If you choose to climb the mountain in an attempt to conquer it, know that the mountain can take your life.

But if it doesn't, and you reach the summit, the mountain will applaud your effort; because it knows that its magnificence and your brilliant endeavor are part of the alchemy of life.

The magnificence of the mountain can be spellbinding. But to hear the mountain applauding YOU … what must that feel like?!"

— Linkedin.com/in/SigiOsagie

***

***

Passion is a unique energy, a special force with purpose.
Ignite and channel yours as rocket fuel for your journey
to career success.

***

Sigi Osagie
@SigiOsagie

Indeed; we are all born the same, and we all have the capacity to achieve extraordinary things. Never let anyone put limits on your dreams or your abilities.

***

"Oftentimes it's the simple things that help the human spirit flourish.

Try to do something simple today that will bring a smile to a face, laughter to a heart and joy to a soul.

That soul could be yours."

— @SigiOsagie

***

The Magic of Self-Leadership

It skipped a few steps along the tree branch, pecking at something I couldn't quite make out. Then it stopped, seemed to look directly at me and puff out its beautiful reddish-orange breast, before breaking into song with a short melody.

I congratulated myself at the good fortune of experiencing this private concert by a solitary robin. But before I knew it, the performance was over.

I watched in fascination as it took off from the branch, flying to a destination I'd never know. Yet somehow, I knew for sure that wherever its flight path was destined for, it would keep singing that song in its heart.

Musing about a robin and its song wasn't what I had headed off to the woods for. But the encounter added a little bit of magic to my morning walk. That robin had seemed so at ease with itself. Perhaps because it doesn't have to worry about a mortgage, utility bills or money for grocery shopping.

Or maybe it's because it doesn't have to contend with an inept boss or a toxic organizational culture that will stifle its song.

Or it could just be because it's able to use its wings to soar to the heights of Olympus to drink with the gods. After all, if you habitually hang out with gods rather than mere mortals or plebs, that's likely to put some swagger in your step; it must instill an unshakable sense of confidence in your psyche.

Few of us are fortunate enough to drink with the gods routinely. But those who do know that to taste the sweet nectar of success you've got to walk the walk by adopting a progressive disposition and effective leadership behaviors.

We often instinctively think that "leadership" is solely about managing others. Yet our ability to manage ourselves as individuals is just as impactful on the performance of our team or organization.

Individuals and their harnessed capabilities are the lifeblood of any organization. So we must embody exceptional standards of self-leadership—the ability to exercise effective leadership over one's self. It starts with knowing yourself. Be aware of who you are, what you stand for, how you think and act, and why you think and act the way you do. This self-insight will help impel you toward the best in you, your personal mojo.

This isn't just about augmenting your contribution to your organization's achievements. It's also about crafting a destiny of success for yourself and polishing your personal brand.

People with strong self-leadership tend to have a deep-seated sense of inner confidence. They're in tune with their inner compass and believe in the magic of themselves; but also appreciate that we're all magicians in our own ways, even though some of us are yet to embrace the power of our individual magic. They routinely leverage the magic of their self-leadership at work, to achieve outstanding levels of performance success and elevate their careers to stellar heights.

When we lack self-leadership, it creates suboptimal work outcomes. Thus, we deny ourselves the opportunity of discovering and revealing our true capabilities. And we deny our organization the opportunity of harnessing the best we can give. Unsurprisingly, our careers suffer.

People with poor self-leadership rarely ever achieve outstanding performance. And work success often seems like drinking at an oasis that is actually a mirage.

Whereas people at the top of their game, who've delivered extraordinary performance and felt their spirit soar to the heights of Olympus, know that the taste of success caresses the palate with a sensation of fulfillment—fulfillment that comes from leading yourself to a veritable oasis.

It's only at the oasis that you can attest that self-leadership is vital for work success. After all, if you can't manage yourself effectively, how can you possibly manage any workplace initiative, project or team successfully?

If you struggle to get this, you'll also struggle to hit your stride.

Those who get it understand how their self-leadership aids their contribution to organizational success, and to the successful development of their own careers. They know that everything they think, say and do impacts their workplace performance and their personal brand.

Whereas those who don't see the light tend to hamper their own effectiveness and tarnish their personal brand through their suboptimal dispositions and regressive behaviors. They'll always be prevented from drinking with the gods by their inadequate self-leadership.

If you are dedicated to strengthening your self-leadership and unleashing your best self, one day the roar of the fire in your belly and the tempo of the song in your heart will compel you to spread your wings and fly—on a flight path destined for the sweet nectar awaiting you at Olympus.

But baby birds don't learn to fly in an instant. It takes repeated and relentless tries. Just as strengthening your self-leadership will. Start with a few things, like:

❖ That unrelenting determination to fly. Taking ownership of your workplace development and career growth, rather than leaving your destiny at the mercy of your organization or your boss, and staying persistent in the face of challenges are fundamental.

❖ This requires heightened personal effectiveness. Which in turn demands clarity of your goals. If your work goals are unclear, then your performance will also be uncertain. And if you have no goals, that's like being on a journey without a destination. If you work for a lousy boss who hasn't set you SMART goals, you must set some yourself—goals that entail a degree of stretch so you can learn and grow.

❖ Maintain a results orientation and hold yourself accountable. Make sure you're delivering results that support your department's aims, the success of your wider organization and your own growth and development—growing from your performance attainments is the reason your goals should be a bit stretching.

❖ Be crystal-clear on what you're responsible for and who you're answerable to, directly or indirectly. And channel your energies at fulfilling your work obligations to a personal standard that is above average. Average standards yield mediocre performance. Outstanding performance comes from unwavering focus, doing the right things for optimal outcomes and staying aware of the impact of your actions on others and vice versa.

❖ Challenge your perspectives by validating that you are going about your work obligations effectively. This includes how you relate to yourself, your boss and your stakeholders. With your boss, you must consider how well you "manage your manager," especially on the communication front. With your colleagues or stakeholders, you must be conscious of the powerful and often hidden influence of emotions in human interactions. And with yourself, you must never doubt the immeasurable capabilities within you.

❖ Take action; with integrity. Intentional action is key to self-leadership. And it's closely correlated to how we use our time. But "time management" is a myth. You cannot "manage" time; what you can manage is yourself—what you do with your time. So spend your time on activities that take you toward your goals in impactful ways. And go about things assertively. (Remember, *assertiveness does not mean aggressiveness!*)

Using your initiative and taking timely and deliberate actions to get what you want is an indispensable habit that will unfurl your wings and help you soar. It's one of the hallmarks of self-leadership. And as your self-leadership expands, so will your wisdom. And more and more, you'll appreciate that you're the architect of your destiny, so you must channel your attention and energy at doing stuff that matters.

For example, you'll increasingly realize that taking intentional action is far more productive for your career success than spending too much time on social media and other digital pursuits which add no value to your destiny. Your expanding self-leadership will expose the perils of becoming derailed and enslaved by your digital gratification.

Digital slavery certainly lurks everywhere in this age, often sapping our personal effectiveness, focus and self-leadership; that's when technology becomes a nemesis rather a valuable tool to use to carve our triumphs.

It's one of the paradoxes of humankind that things that are good for us (e.g., in the beneficial ways we can leverage them) can sometimes be bad for us too (e.g., when we become fixated with them). Like an artist who becomes fixated with his palettes or paintbrushes, forgetting that they're simply tools of his trade; his vocation is still to create paintings—that's where his focus should be.

Rather than be hijacked and enslaved by technology, it's pivotal to our work success and career growth to stay attuned to our inner drives, dreams and desires. So always remain alert to how much time and attention you spend on social media versus how much time and attention you spend listening to the song in your heart.

Sometimes we delude ourselves that our technology addiction or social media gluttony is providing us with learning; no doubt, from the plethora of online sources now available. Perhaps it's because the internet has made everyone an expert or guru on everything. Beware of social media prophets with proverbs, promises and platitudes. Check to validate robust proof of their miracles before buying into their religion.

Your expanding self-leadership will also highlight to you that social media addiction isn't the only way technology can enslave us and drown out the melody of our song. Email is another.

Many of us have unknowingly developed the habit of *instantly* checking, replying to or taking action on emails. And it's definitely not the most effective way to work. Nor is it characteristic of meaningful self-leadership.

Emails may have become a poison to our personal effectiveness and productivity, much like social media gluttony.

My own antidote to the poison is to constantly remind myself that the time is exactly "XYZ" time on "ABC" day and I'll never get this moment in my life again. I get one shot at it; so I must use it wisely—on things that take me toward my goals, as I have planned.

Of course, those goals can be varied. If the goal is pleasure, then spending the XYZ time with my mistress is priority. If the goal is serenity, then a walk in the woods might be what I invest the time in. If the goal is to hone my voodoo magic skills, then the time is spent in my voodoo shrine …

So it all comes down to the goals we're targeting; planning ahead how to spend our time to realize those goals; and the self-discipline to stick to the plan, despite the constant pings of new emails or social media alerts.

If our goals are powerful and motivating enough, the pull of the pings and alerts will likely be suppressed by the allure of working toward attaining the goals.

So, are your goals powerful and motivating enough?

Or, put another way, is your "castle" magnificent enough to capture and retain your full focus?

Alternatively, what do you do: do you let the poison get you, or do you have a different antidote?

Whatever your approach, always remember that being a puppet jumping to the summons of pings and alerts is not self-leadership in practice; rather, it *is* being led by something other than yourself, a behavioral cocaine of sorts.

Sometimes our drug dealers supplying the cocaine can be the people we spend time with in our private lives—when our unproductive behaviors or outlook on life simply mimic or are heavily influenced by theirs, and we're blind to the negative impacts that has on our effectiveness, growth and career success.

At other times our cocaine dealers may be the very organizations we work in—when the organizational climate or prevalent culture tunnels our vision and outlook; or when we allow ourselves to become organizational clones, embracing and mirroring thinking or behavioral patterns which neither serve us in achieving our objectives in an effective manner nor aid the fulfillment of our career aspirations.

You mustn't let the organizational culture you work in (big-company culture, small-business mentality, or whatever) make you lose sight of who you are, the sort of person or professional you aspire to be and what you truly want from your career.

You may need to be flexible and learn to deal with some hogwash in the workplace. That flexibility is strength. Being able to fluidly adapt your approach or work style—without discarding your authentic self—helps you deal with a broader range of circumstances and personalities in your life and career; a bit like the flexible trees that are more able to withstand the storms because they can bend and sway with the wind. But ultimately, if the job or organization you're in doesn't match your values and aspirations or diminishes your happiness, doing something about it *is* self-leadership in action.

So is owning your mistakes as well as your victories.

And holding yourself liable for your career growth and success.

You are the one who must decide what's important to you and who/how you want to be in your career, and go about your work and your life accordingly.

Aside from the many cocaine dealers in life constantly touting their wares to entice us into a career of eventual mediocrity, many of us struggle with embodying effective self-leadership because we want to eat the ripe, juicy fruit without cultivating the plant that bears the fruit.

I was one of those. Before I learned that you have to practice self-leadership to enhance your self-leadership.

Make a commitment to yourself. And keep it. Because you acknowledge that your career is important to you, and you're determined to make a success of it; because your dreams matter.

And no matter how many times you "fail" at practicing or how "hard" it seems, keep trying.

Just keep trying.

Persistently.

And consistently.

The more you keep trying, the more you amplify your chances of success—it's always the same with creating or embracing new habits, thinking patterns or behaviors: the more you practice, the more ingrained the habit becomes.

Making a commitment as such and giving it your all—despite any challenges, disruptions or disillusionment you may experience—is another example of self-leadership in action. And the book you hold in your hand is filled with many others.

So, don't just read the advice and tips in this book; put them into practice to equip and empower yourself to boost your career success.

As you make progress on your career journey, you must be clear on what your own definition of that "success" is. Your career success shouldn't be defined by or measured against what others do or achieve. You should be more influenced by your own desires, convictions, actions and results than by the opinions or attainments of other people.

Other people are not living your life, dreaming your dreams or experiencing your career. You are.

And other people may never know of the power of the magic inside you. You will.

Self-leadership is about discovering your inner magic and harnessing it for your success. It demands knowing more about your true self—how you tick and how to get the best out of you. That knowledge will help you achieve your career dreams when you apply it.

It's a bit like learning more about one of your staff so you can manage them better, and help them contribute more, develop more and fulfill their potential; that staff is you.

Like every one of us, you can always lead yourself to drink with the gods at Olympus, the same gods who ordain your personal success—because you were born with that capacity in you.

Have faith in yourself. And don't let anyone stop you. Your sweet nectar awaits you!

Nuggets for Your Success

***

Leadership is partly about getting someone to do what they need to do (and may not want to do) to achieve what they want to accomplish—that someone could be you.

***

***

We only have one life to live. And we'll spend most of that time at work. We owe it to ourselves to embody exceptional standards of self-leadership to unleash the best in us; because life is not a dress rehearsal.

***

***

Self-leadership is essential to proactively develop and nurture personal capabilities.

***

***

Self-leadership demands the inner discipline and strength to do things because they are the right things to do, even if your actions make you unpopular; and the self-regulation of monitoring and managing your thinking, feelings and behaviors so they are conducive to the outcomes you desire.

***

***

Ask yourself this: Do I embody effective self-leadership in my thinking and day-to-day activities?

***

***

"If you venture into the jungle without adequate preparation, you can't blame anyone else for whatever ills befall you.

Having at least some idea of your game plan for YOUR #careersuccess is imperative."

— @SigiOsagie

***

***

"Learning from books, gurus, electronic media and other sources is great. Yet we can only ever truly learn about some things by doing them or experiencing them.

And other things, we can only learn from the sage within us."

— @SigiOsagie

***

Sigi Osagie
@SigiOsagie

. . .

Have YOU got oomph?
Or are you compromising your
#career destiny by staying put
with a #leader or an
organization that doesn't
bring out the best in you?

> **People with oomph
> seldom stay with leaders or
> organizations that don't
> bring out the best in them.**
>
> **sigi**OSAGIE
> *Delivers Effectiveness & Performance Growth*
>
> © Sigi Osagie, 2014
> **www.sigiosagie.com**

Sigi Osagie
@SigiOsagie

"We should each play our own game — be who we are & be true to ourselves.

But, sadly, many of us are held back by our 'scripts' & our fears. And we go thro' life never really discovering & harnessing the immeasurable capabilities within us."

Sigi Osagie　　　···

Writer, Speaker, Business Adviser & Coach +
Mentor. Author, SWEET STAKEHOLDER
LOVE, and other books to up your game
4y

Sage advice on #leadership.
Of course, the most important person you lead
is yourself. So it applies to your self-leadership
too. Listen to yourself and watch yourself —
your thoughts, your actions and your emotions;
you'll be astounded by the learning that'll
emerge. But it'll be learning that'll help you rock
to a sweeter tempo.

> "If you are leading people, it helps to
> have a sense of who they are... the
> actions that will draw out the best in
> them,... The only way to figure this out is
> by two underrated activities: listening
> and watching."
>
> – Sir Alex Ferguson
> in *Leading* with Sir Michael Moritz

Sigi Osagie   ▪ ▪ ▪
Writer, Speaker, Business Adviser & Coach +
Mentor. Author, SWEET STAKEHOLDER
LOVE, and other books to up your game
4y · Edited

What did you want to be when you grew up?
Firefighter? Astronaut? Policeman/woman?
Teacher? Doctor? Dancer? Pilot? Voodoo
Priest/Priestess?...

I'm still growing up.
And when I grow up I want to be like the birds:
to sing my song without caring who "Likes" it.

What DO you want to be when you grow up?

76

***

"The bird spends all day flying, because the bird was born to fly; and it knows that.

The fish spends all day swimming, because the fish was born to swim; and it also knows that.

What do you spend all day doing, and what were you born to do? Do you know?

Many of us have lost track of the song in our hearts and simply roll with the prevailing winds, conform to convention or the expectations of others, or follow the crowd we find ourselves in. But your true desires remain somewhere deep in your heart.

Just be brave enough to look.

And as you contemplate whatever you find, and subsequently endeavor to craft your career destiny, remember that our hearts know us better than we know ourselves; and our hearts have skin in our game too. So it's useful to also 'think' with your heart, even if only every now and then."

— @SigiOsagie

***

Words and Silence

WHAT AN ENTHRALLING EXPERIENCE!

I was still thinking about it and smiling to myself in delight, some ten minutes or so later, as I ambled across the old wooden bridge that spanned the little creek meandering through the woods.

The appearance of that great tit and the harmonic notes it had belted out right in front of me was a wondrous occurrence that spiced up my walk even more; it brought something inexplicable and sublime, infusing me with more magic and delight than I'd been feeling.

It was particularly noteworthy because it was the second such gift I had enjoyed that morning. Just a few minutes before, I'd had the good fortune to encounter another solitary bird, one that was just as much a virtuoso performer. Seeing the robin so close by had stopped me in my tracks.

I was exhilarated at the double blessing of two private concerts by two spectacular birds. And it got me thinking about the number "2," and how our life is so filled with the duality it represents—so many things with two aspects to them or two contrasting elements: good and bad, night and day, yin and yang, pleasure and pain, fast and slow, love and hate, …

This ever-present dualism is probably most pronounced in our everyday lives in the contrast between the words we use when we speak and the silence we experience when we don't speak.

Words are tremendously powerful, whether they are expressed in the mind, spoken with the tongue, written with the pen or typed with a keyboard.

Words carry energy that can bring joy or misery, can evoke laughter or tears, can lift people up or tear them down. Sweet words of love by lyricists and crooners like Barry White have led to the creation of many new little humans all over the world. And poisonous words of hate by tyrants and evil zealots have led to the destruction of millions of human lives through the ages. Because words transmit impact.

So it's crucial to watch your choice of words in everyday conversations—for example, with colleagues and stakeholders at work, with contacts in your career network and with yourself.

Always remember that the words you use in your mind or your self-talk paint and shape your "reality," ultimately.

You're also adding hues of color and configuration to others' reality when you interact with them. If they perceive your vibe and communication unfavorably, it's detrimental to your personal brand, a key underpinning of your career success.

You're more likely to attune someone you're interacting with if you first listen attentively to them. Listening candidly can be a great doorway to reading other people better and sensing their true sentiments, so you can choose and package your own words to resonate with them.

This isn't just about what you say. Like everyone else, your non-verbal communication or body language accounts for well over fifty percent of your communication. *How* you say it can be as important as, if not more important than, what you say.

When we speak, things like our posture, facial expressions, gestures and tone of voice convey more than we may be aware of, and may transmit what we don't intend to communicate. Yet it can be far worse or better when we don't speak at all.

Effective communication is a crucial competence for career success. And knowing when and how to speak and when and how to be silent is a cornerstone of communicating constructively with others, and more importantly, with ourselves.

Silence, at the right moments, even if just a brief pause, is a potent communication device that can sometimes achieve more than words. It also helps us listen better and retain more of what is being transmitted to us—whether the transmitter is a colleague at work, a loved one at home or the sage within us. So our chances of capturing and benefiting from every morsel of the communication to us increase significantly.

Many of us are scared of silence though; we may not be sedatephobic but we sure do avoid it often enough. And we may not admit our aversion or even be aware of it. Yet we can each verify this by observing our choices and actions in our everyday doings.

Our fear or avoidance of silence is one of those inconspicuous, little day-to-day things that detract from our personal effectiveness, productivity, work success and fulfillment. Because those everyday choices and actions nourish or tarnish our mojo.

Perhaps we avoid silence because something in us (our ego?) feels that silence is an empty nothingness.

It's easy to be fooled into thinking that silence is empty. It isn't.

Silence is a vessel of wisdom.

And its potency can be much greater than the power of words.

It's in silence that we hear the call of the dreams of our hearts clearer and louder. A call that steers us to our destiny, if we have the courage and confidence to answer it.

It's in silence that we fully perceive and comprehend what people are truly communicating to us, especially the stuff between the words, stuff that remains unspoken and often holds more insight than the words themselves; or perceive and comprehend the broadcast from our inner guru, trying to aid our efforts to realize our dreams.

It's in silence that we're perfectly able to distinguish between words and other perceptions that are merely "noise" and those that hold valuable truths, understanding and wisdom.

And it's in silence that we appreciate the criticality of not succumbing to the seduction of perceptions that hold no value, like empty, meaningless words—which may be expressed by others or by ourselves.

Silence enables and empowers us to filter out the worthless and meaningless stuff, the noise; especially in today's world, cluttered as it is with distractions, ineffectiveness and the games people play.

And whenever we're able to fade out the noise, even if only for short spells, we harness perhaps the greatest virtue of silence: perceiving the gigantic river of knowledge in us with clarity, a river from which we can drink infinitely to leverage a knowledge beyond reason. Each sip of the drink helps expose our best self and expands our capabilities, including our ability to choose and shape the right string of words; words which then create our desired impact by accurately conveying what we truly wish to transmit—whether the receiver is a colleague at work, a loved one at home or our authentic self.

It's funny how silence can lead us to finding and using the right words. And actions. And choices.

And in the end, it's those choices and actions that sculpt our career destiny.

Every Time We Say Goodbye

THE SAGES SAY THAT LIFE is created in each moment. Every moment we spend interacting with colleagues and stakeholders at work is an opportunity to build positive perceptions of our personal brand and the team or organization we represent.

Whether these interactions occur in formal meetings or informal corridor conversations is less important than the realization that such moments pass quickly. And before we know it we're saying goodbye.

Do we ever stop to consider what we leave behind every time we say goodbye?

The moments we spend with our colleagues and stakeholders give us the prospect of cultivation. These moments are fertile grounds upon which we can sow seeds of misunderstanding, confrontation and all sorts of negative sentiments.

Or we can choose to use those moments to sprinkle gold dust, and cultivate a different set of emotions and perceptions more conducive to our organizational well-being, our work performance and, ultimately, our career success.

People who are highly effective operators are very aware of what they're cultivating from moment to moment. But for many of us, unschooled in such matters though highly proficient in the technical aspects of our jobs, we may often only realize what we've sown when we come to say goodbye—the responses and body language of the person(s) we've been interacting with are typical telltale signs.

Quite often, we sow the wrong seeds or read the signs wrongly simply because we may be handicapped by our own personal bias; because our perspectives on all aspects of life are shaped by the environments we've grown up in, biologically and professionally, and the "scripts" we've picked up from others in those environments.

The scripts are the *subliminal* programming of our worldviews—our beliefs, values and how we perceive and interpret life, including our work life. And most of us are not even aware of this.

For instance, some managers who spend their formative professional years in organizations where autocratic leadership prevails end up embodying similar regressive, bully-boy leadership styles when they themselves become senior leaders. It's the old "monkey see, monkey do" syndrome.

These professionals unknowingly develop a flawed script of what effective leadership means, and end up carrying this imprint throughout their careers; unless they are subsequently exposed to other, more progressive environmental influences and make concerted efforts to rewrite their scripts.

In the same way, someone might have grown up in Kinshasa in the Democratic Republic of the Congo but may now be living and working in Kentucky in the USA; their worldview—and consequently, their attitudes and behaviors at work—is quite likely to be strongly influenced by the script of their cultural and societal upbringing in Congo. They'll need to be conscious of this and make whatever adjustments they deem necessary if they are to thrive in their professional career in the USA.

Or similarly, someone may come from a part of the world where educational qualifications are the be-all and end-all for career growth and progression, perhaps even more so than experience. Yet they may now be developing their career in another part of the world and in a field where networking, people smarts or personality traits may be more critical for success; they'll need to rejig their perspective and up their game accordingly to assure their career prosperity.

Becoming aware of how our environments and related scripts influence our thinking, perspectives and actions is one of the most powerful learning experiences for anyone. It's a key aid to expanding our personal effectiveness, and has an indelible impact on our work accomplishments and career success.

It's particularly relevant to our interactions with colleagues and stakeholders, who may be just as challenged or stressed out by the incessant hustle and bustle of the modern-day workplace as we are.

The more self-aware we become, the better we're able to recognize why individual stakeholders may not see things as we do.

This divergence of views can easily become a stumbling block that prevents us from selling our work agenda successfully and winning people over.

I've learned from experience (sometimes painful!) that winning people over demands that I take the trouble to understand individuals better. Gaining that deeper understanding requires a paradigm shift, moving from my own script and predispositions to seeing and thinking differently.

By creating different mental models and thus shifting our perspectives, we enable and empower ourselves to perceive and behave in more productive ways which we may have been blinded to by our scripts.

I often use a simple card exercise with coaching and mentoring clients to illustrate the concept of shifting perspectives. If I hold a normal business card up to you and ask you what you see, you will probably describe it as "a business card," and perhaps read out what the card says—the name, job title, company and so on. But I, on the other side of the card, will see something different: a blank card on the reverse side. Yet we'd both be looking at the same card.

Of course, if we swap positions each of us will then be able to see what the other had seen. So it is with shifting perspectives—it's really about seeing things from different viewpoints; and recognizing that our scripts are always at play, typically impelling our predispositions to particular perspectives.

The business card exercise is a simple illustration of the interplay of scripting, perspective and self-awareness, and how those dynamics impact our ability to understand others and nurture productive work relationships; relationships which help to oil the wheels of our career success.

We can be more effective in our careers if we seek to understand work colleagues and stakeholders first before pushing our own agenda.

Adopting this approach helps us recognize that we may only ever be perceiving or considering "one side of the business card," or one or two aspects of what is often a multifaceted work issue, task or project.

This insight is tightly linked to our personal intelligence as individuals; not least our ability to comprehend our own scripts, which are often deep-seated, playing out at a subconscious level and influencing our perceptions, choices and actions—and consequently, our career destinies. The more we enhance this self-awareness, the better we become at self-leadership, a foundational prerequisite for work and career success.

The many moments we spend with colleagues and stakeholders provide ample opportunities to grow our self-awareness and up our game. So every time you end an interaction and say goodbye, ask yourself what you left behind: did you sow seeds of negative sentiments or did you sprinkle gold dust?

Nuggets for Your Success

***

Our scripts are highly potent forces that influence our personal bias and predispositions, thus impacting most aspects of our lives, including our work and careers.

***

***

If you're technically competent at your job or well versed in your field but go about things in a way that damages your stakeholder relationships, you're harming your personal effectiveness and long-term career success.

Remember that whatever your colleagues, stakeholders and contacts in your network outside the workplace think, feel and say about you impacts your reputation, and consequently, your workplace success and career prospects.

***

***

Do you know the hidden script that shapes *your* work and career success? Can you identify specific elements of it?

Making efforts to edit your script and create a more beneficial version will aid your career growth immensely.

***

Sigi Osagie
@SigiOsagie

"THE POWER OF WORDS and THE POTENCY OF SILENCE have a phenomenal impact on your #personaleffectiveness, #productivity, work success and fulfillment.": bit.ly/3Ekz7iG

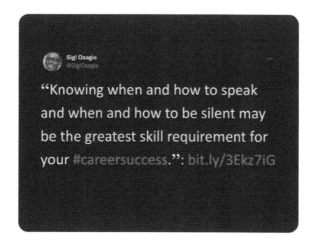

"Knowing when and how to speak and when and how to be silent may be the greatest skill requirement for your #careersuccess.": bit.ly/3Ekz7iG

***

"The ability to fade out the noise and tune into yourself is greatly undervalued amongst the arsenal of skills the modern-day professional needs. Yet it's a core requirement for effective self-leadership and enduring success."
— @SigiOsagie

***

Sigi Osagie
@SigiOsagie

To tap the inner wisdom life bestows on every one of us, we must stay open to new ways of seeing, perceiving, thinking and acting.

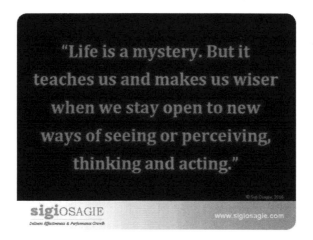

"Life is a mystery. But it teaches us and makes us wiser when we stay open to new ways of seeing or perceiving, thinking and acting."

sigiOSAGIE

www.sigiosagie.com

***

Your character, ethics and personal brand reputation are all crucial factors which impact your credibility; and hence have an indelible bearing on your career destiny.

And your personal brand profile—the perception people have of you and your vibe, not your perception of yourself—is largely based on its positioning in the minds of your colleagues, stakeholders and contacts in your career network. You must be savvy and effective with your interactions so that their perceptions and sentiments about you are always admirable; which goes a long way to oil the wheels of your progress and advancement, perpetually getting you closer to achieving your career dreams.

Always remember that every touchpoint you have with people, at work and throughout your career journey, can tarnish or burnish your brand.

Never forget how important this is for your workplace success and long-term career growth.

***

***

One of the most momentous touchpoints for anyone is the first impression we convey to others. This doesn't necessarily happen in person or by direct interaction; impressions can be formed second-hand through other people and various indirect channels, e.g., your CV or social media profile, an email you send or a presentation you give.

Even when we're not aware, people are constantly having a sniff of us as new acquaintances and forming early impressions—though it isn't always nor totally done in a conscious way. And it happens quite quickly; we tend to appraise people and make up our minds about them in a few moments.

Of course, those initial judgments aren't always correct. But they frequently hold a reasonable dose of accuracy, as proven by research.

First impressions can have strong, lasting impacts on how people perceive you and relate to you. And shifting negative first impressions can be difficult. So starting out with the impression you want to give is imperative. It's a fundamental component of cultivating a personal brand that augments your career success.

***

***

Another important yet obscure touchpoint for you is what people hear you say about others.

It can be very tempting to say derogatory things about a work colleague or someone else in your career network, especially if you're having difficulties with them. But it's probably best to not give in to the temptation.

Bad-mouthing anyone just doesn't contribute anything positive to your relationship with them.

Naturally, you can discuss your difficulties with trusted colleagues, friends or family members. Getting things off your chest or venting into a listening ear can be helpful to relieve emotional pressure, and getting some perspective from others can expand your perceptions and understanding and aid your capacity to deal with the difficulty more effectively. Such exchanges may be good for your mojo, when the discussion isn't centered on poisoning the air with words that harm another human spirit—which is what bad-mouthing is; a toxic and infectious activity that erodes your credibility and integrity as a professional. It hurts the reputation of the other person. And in the long run, it'll likely hurt yours too and damage your personal brand.

***

***

"So many hidden gems of wisdom in the simple message by Angela Ahrendts—especially for managers/leaders who try to create clones of themselves in their people, or organizations who espouse such an ethos (sometimes, un-wittingly), or, worse still, those of us who allow ourselves to be cloned and lose sight of who we really are.

Always remember that YOU are unique—God (or Allah, Yahweh, Nature, Big Bang, Ahura Mazda, … whatever you believe in) made you as YOU for a reason. Be true to yourself."

— Linkedin.com/in/SigiOsagie

***

***

"Conversation with a Visitor at My Voodoo Magic Shrine

VISITOR:
Sigi, why do you keep talking about 'listening to the song in your heart,' and what is this song anyway?

MOI:
The song in your heart is the only song there is, really. And it's sweeter than anything on the radio, YouTube or SoundCloud.

Yet when you listen to it, you'll hear a line in there that implores you to also acknowledge the songs emanating from others' hearts.

It's the skillful blend of your song with others' that creates #career success, like the sweet music a maestro creates by drawing on various elements of the orchestra.

You have to shape your own career destiny. But no successful person on the planet ever achieved their success entirely of their own accord. We're all 'carried' in various ways—sometimes unseen or unexplainable—by others, e.g., through advice, encouragement, help, opportunities, good wishes, support, challenges or love.

As you endeavor to craft your #careersuccess, remember to surround yourself with people who can help you flourish. And draw on their support and nourishment; just as much as you provide the same to others."

— Linkedin.com/in/SigiOsagie

***

***

"There are few things more rewarding than helping
another human spirit to flourish."
— Linkedin.com/in/SigiOsagie

***

***

"Nobody will sing YOUR song for you, because they don't know the lyrics and the tempo.

When YOU 'write' the lyrics and start singing yourself, then you may find others who'll join in your song to create a beautiful melody."
— Linkedin.com/in/SigiOsagie

***

***

"In times to come, some people will be sharing stories and legends about some great people and the magnificent successes they achieved. Which group of people will you be in?"

— @SigiOsagie

***

An Incompetent Boss

LEADERSHIP IS THE SINGLE MOST important factor affecting people's motivation, performance and success at work. Consequently, more than likely, your boss is your most important colleague or stakeholder.

Working for an incompetent boss is a challenge many people face at some point in their careers—people like Martin S., who sent me this query:

"What if your leadership has no idea what they're doing, has zero relevant experience and knowledge and no plans?"

My feedback:

Although it's not often publicized, this can be a debilitating problem for many people. In the worst cases, working for a leader who is seemingly clueless can make you feel like jumping out of a tenth-floor window and slitting your throat on the way down.

In less severe cases, where your boss hasn't engaged and inspired the team, it can still be demoralizing.

Either way, working for an incompetent or ineffective boss can become a source of stress.

People sometimes undervalue the vital importance of effective leadership in the workplace. Yet leadership is the glue that holds it all together. That's why the best organizations invest significantly in their leadership bench strength, and ensure incumbent leaders embody leadership styles that get the best from their people.

Managers at all levels are the critical conduits to nourishing the psychological contract between employees and the organization.

Unfortunately, Martin, we don't all work for top-notch organizations. And we sometimes end up working for leaders we have no faith in. It can be a multifaceted issue, so let's focus on some of the most important elements, particularly those within your control.

Firstly, are you referring to your functional or department leader specifically, or the organizational leadership collectively?

If it's the latter, then it may be that you're in the wrong environment. You can't change the leadership capability in your organization. So don't drive yourself insane by trying. Life is too short to spend a huge chunk of it in toxic organizational environments. You should find a job in an organization whose values and ethos align with yours. (Of course, you must know what your own values are.)

If it's your department or functional leader specifically, my guidance is to retain focus on your effectiveness and job success; that means doing the right things right.

Confront your thinking and discernment by attesting that you yourself are meeting your responsibilities and obligations competently. This may include how you communicate with your boss; and indeed, if and how you provide feedback to them on pertinent work issues, including their leadership approach. You should be doing this assertively and politely.

You should also validate your perceptions by observing your boss in a structured way for a few days or weeks. Try to be objective in your observations and identify specific examples of what they do right and wrong, and the positive or negative aspects of their leadership approach.

At the same time, see if you can identify your boss's motivational drivers. This is an invaluable aid to understanding them better and learning to "manage your manager" more effectively.

If you have trusted colleagues in the team, you may tactfully check your perceptions with their opinions to confirm your views.

Irrespective of your viewpoint and feelings, it may be valuable to have an honest one-to-one dialogue with your boss.

You should approach this with candor, tact and assertiveness. Your earlier structured observations may come in useful to exemplify points you raise in the discussion. It'd be prudent to take notes at this meeting. And remember that listening to them empathetically is as important as stating your case. So listen well to what they say and, perhaps more importantly, what they don't say.

Being an effective listener is something we should all strive for. And it's particularly relevant in important discussions like this. Trying to assimilate people's communication and grasp their rationale requires giving them your full attention as if they're the center of your world. It also requires listening with your ears, your heart, as well as your behavior—for example, by maintaining good eye contact without being awkward, and using gestures, like a nod, or phrases like "Okay," "I get you" or "I agree" to reinforce what they're communicating. Voicing your agreement with specific statements they make, even if you disagree with their overall stance or opinion, can sometimes convey solid reassurance that you indeed comprehend what's being relayed to you, which can only help the dialogue.

Listening effectively means you should also pay close attention to their body language. Reading the countless non-verbal cues people emit—deliberately or reflexively—can sometimes reveal more than the words they speak.

Listening is a cornerstone of understanding others. Listening to your own self—your inner voice, what you say and how you say it—also helps you grow your self-awareness and cultivate a mindset that'll help you deal with challenges such as an ineffective manager.

It's important to maintain the right frame of mind to navigate through these sorts of workplace issues. Don't allow negative emotions to hijack you or your career destiny.

Your mindset or outlook may help you recognize that, as challenging as it may be, dealing with an incompetent boss is also an opportunity to learn and grow. We only grow when we stretch beyond what we can do already. Stretching your capabilities to deal with your boss effectively will help you learn how to handle other similar challenges in your future career.

And if you've got oomph, which I presume you do, you'll climb high. The higher you climb, the more likely you'll face challenges of some sort.

Seeing the situation as a growth opportunity is helpful even if you opt to leave the organization. Deciding to leave may make you feel justified to make a formal complaint to your HR department. Nonetheless, I'd caution that making a formal complaint should be your last resort—when you feel you've exhausted all other avenues.

One avenue to consider is talking things over confidentially with an experienced and trustworthy senior manager in your organization. Another is changing jobs and moving to a different area of the organization, if possible. Again, it's important to have clarity of your long-term aspirations so that such a move is still in line with your career goals.

Keeping your focus on your job/career success and your personal effectiveness is crucial. Ultimately, whatever tactics help address the issue, you owe it to yourself to take responsibility for shaping your immediate job context and career destiny, such that you can thrive and shine.

Don't let your destiny be held to ransom by an incompetent boss. And if you currently manage people, or will do in future, let your experience with this situation help you yourself be a fantastic boss to work for.

Moving up the Ladder

ONE OF THE MANY CHALLENGES professionals struggle with is mastering how to grow their careers successfully— people like Thomas D., who sent me this query:

"I've got many years' experience working in Procurement roles in different companies, and I consider myself to be a good Procurement manager. But I still haven't been able to step up to a senior or executive-level role as I would like. What do you see as the most important skill I need to make that move up?

Also, I worked in the public sector for a few years before moving into the private sector. Now I'm thinking of moving back to the public sector, and I want to do a master's degree, partly to help me transition back in—I'm not sure which one to go with between Master of Commerce, MSc in Supply Chain Management, Master of Public Administration and MBA. What's your advice?"

My feedback:
Regarding the first part of your enquiry, it's less about being in Procurement than about moving up the career ladder. You could be in Finance, Marketing, Project Management, Engineering, Voodoo Department or any other functional area and still face the same challenge; everyone with some ambition wants to move up the ladder, whether the ladder is in Procurement or any other field.

It's an issue many people ponder but never really take action to address.

Sometimes people don't feel confident enough to ask; or they may have no one—a mentor, coach, shaman or whatever—to explore the issue with and get the career development help they need.

Or worse still, some people just continue to bumble along without any thought given to their career growth and direction.

I presume that you're currently in a middle-level role. This clarification is important, as the skills needed in middle management can be quite different from those required to step up to a senior management role.

In the same way, the skills needed in a senior management role may be slightly different from the competencies required for an executive role or the C-suite.

I hope your "many years' experience" means several years spent in different roles building a broad knowledge base and multiple perspectives. This distinction is also important—you should grow your career experience from different stints of work, rather than doing the same thing time and again with no expansion of your competencies and prowess. Some people have "10 years' experience," for example, but it's actually one year's experience times 10. This is not growth.

You consider yourself to be "a good Procurement manager," which may be correct. But being "good" may not be adequate to make the step up. Good often means average or same as most people. What you want is not to be good but to be outstanding; you'll find it easier to make the step up compared to many others who are good or average.

There isn't really one "most important skill" required to move up to a senior role, other than your personal effectiveness. This is the single trait or competence that affects everything else.

For instance, your personal effectiveness shows in your ability to think clearly about your intents: you must be clear on your career goal(s) and what "success" looks like to you. Does success mean a big pay check, a massive corner office, a retinue of first-line reports overseeing a huge empire of underlings for you; or the freedom to come and go as you please, spending your time on work tasks entirely of your choosing; or doing work that brings the joys of spring to your soul and sets your heart a-dancing; or living in a state of inner peace and fulfillment; or what? Is your aspiration to step up into an Operations, Supply Chain or General Management senior leadership role, for example, or to become a Chief Procurement Officer or Chief Operating Officer?

Each of these (and other executive roles) may require different routes. You may need to get some exposure to other functional areas beyond your current field, Procurement.

You could do this in any number of ways—such as getting a secondment to another area; learning from colleagues in other functions; working on company projects that will give you significant exposure to the workings of other departments; making a deliberate job change to another function.

If your decided approach entails a job move, consider it as a stepping stone toward your ultimate career goal.

Of course, what you learn from any such job move may also impact your subsequent perspectives on your career, and hence your goals.

Broadening your experience base will give you a more rounded understanding of business and the wider organization, and a better grasp of the implications of each function's actions on other functional areas, which will help develop your strategic thinking and awareness. This is always advantageous in executive roles, even if you remain in Procurement.

I've deliberately drawn on your own words to give you some pointers. So I hope you can see that your ability to step up to a senior role starts with your own perspectives—how you see yourself and your worldview.

That viewpoint should include a recognition that your career is made up of a series of jobs or vocations. If you make your job choices or career moves with proper reflection and consideration of your long-term aspirations, and you make a success of each individual job you do, then you're on your way. Doing your current job brilliantly well is one of the best things you can do to shape your long-term career success.

A master's degree can indeed aid your career growth and success. It's a big and commendable academic achievement.

It should be undertaken for the right reasons though.

For example, how exactly do you see it serving as a transition back into the public sector for you? Have you done any research or investigations that indicate that having a master's degree helps in this way *in your particular context* (e.g., in your country, in your professional field or the functional area you aspire to be in, for the sort of senior-level jobs you desire); and if so, does your research identify any particular master's qualification as being more advantageous?

It's imperative to ascertain what a master's degree would add to your career development or how it'd help in attaining your goals or aspirations.

You mustn't do it based on misguided thinking, nor for inappropriate reasons, e.g., because it's the in thing, or because your family expect you to, or because it was specified as a requirement for one or two advertised jobs you fancied, or because it'd look impressive on your CV or social media profile.

You need to judge the overall necessity of doing a master's and, if appropriate, make a choice between the options based on your long-term career goals or life plan.

Whether you do a master's degree or not, you should focus your career development efforts on expanding your skills set.

For anyone aspiring to move up to senior leadership/executive roles (rather than becoming solely a functional specialist, for example), this is less about technical skills and more about what it takes to step up and stay up: soft skills.

It's not your technical expertise that will propel you upwards. Your technical competencies are simply "Qualifiers"—they qualify you to play in the Procurement sandpit, like thousands or millions of others. But it's your soft skills that will differentiate you, help you excel and win in your career—they are your "Order Winners."

People with poor soft skills typically have stunted careers.

The higher up you climb, the more vital your soft skills become. And you're more likely to grow wings and fly if you get yourself a mentor or coach to help you sharpen those abilities.

Getting a sponsor in your organization may also help in that regard. A sponsor is more likely to put the wind in your sails by being a proactive advocate for your visibility and advancement. For example, they'll open doors for you, put your name forward, connect you to the right people for appropriate opportunities and do what they can to help you succeed and move up. A good sponsor is of inestimable value, especially in large organizations.

Other than your personal effectiveness, some critical soft skills to hone include:

❖ Self-leadership. You must be adept at managing yourself—how you think, what you focus on, how you act, and so on. This includes effective use of your time and energy.

❖ People management. In a line management role you must be effective at getting the best out of your people. Engaging and aligning people effectively is also important to get results through others who don't report to you.

❖ Results orientation. Focus on delivering results; that's what you're paid for. If your boss hasn't defined your objectives, do so yourself—make them SMART. Then deliver.

❖ Persuasive communication and influence. Sharpen your abilities to win people over. This isn't just about using hard facts and technical lingo; get savvy at connecting with folks emotionally and listening empathetically.

❖ Interpersonal relationships. Continually propagate healthy work relationships. Immerse yourself in appropriate networks of people who will have positive impacts on your growth. Always remember The Golden Rule, and help others when you can.

❖ Brand management. Make yourself visible, and manage your personal brand sensibly. Learn how to build rapport, communicate your achievements and aspirations, and market yourself; in the right way, to the right audience and with the right message.

Managing your personal brand is an intrinsic aspect of selling yourself effectively—and more so as regards moving up and staying up at senior levels.

This isn't about being a vainglorious twit, brown-nosing or becoming a yes-man or a political animal. Rather, it's about making people aware of your positive traits (e.g., through your operating style, the way you come across as a person and your proactive efforts to network and foster camaraderie) and the value you bring to your work and the organization (e.g., by blowing your own trumpet with subtlety and finesse).

Mercedes-Benz don't invest effort in making a brilliant car and then tell no one about it. So if you're brilliant at your work, a solid contributor, have desirable traits and experience, and get on well with people, you should exhibit that; albeit with the right degree of modesty.

You're selling yourself when you write your accomplishments on your CV or a job application form. And you have to sell yourself at interviews to get the job. Why might you think selling yourself stops there?

You also have to sell yourself throughout your career—for instance, to secure better opportunities, pay increases or promotions—in order to get wherever you want to be ultimately.

Career success involves lots of selling.

The idea of "selling yourself" might have a negative connotation for you; it often triggers an instinctive mental recoil in many of us. Maybe because it immediately sounds pushy, distasteful or unappealing. It probably conjures up images of a snake-oil salesman with low ethical standards. Yet, if you think about it deeply, much of our everyday work entails some form of selling, not least every instance of asking our managers, colleagues or stakeholders to consider or accept a different perspective or a new angle on some work issue or another.

We may not have to work hard at selling the different perspective or new angle. But the very fact that it's new or different means that, more often than not, there's inherently some element of "selling" involved in people "buying" into and accepting our ideas.

The notion of an inherent element of selling in our work is something you have to recognize and embrace to be successful in the workplace, especially if your definition of success includes climbing up the career ladder; because we're selling almost all the time, knowingly or unknowingly—selling ourselves, our personal brand, ideas, visions, projects, new practices, and so on, to our staff, our bosses, our peers and our stakeholders.

In fact, life itself entails lots of selling and buying.

For example, right from childhood our parents sell us a rubric of morality and, generally speaking, we buy into it; we sell our best selves to love interests, who buy into the potential happiness and sweetness we convey and end up as our spouses and lovers; prophets, gurus and all manner of religions sell us doctrines and beliefs which we buy into; even your boss or employer sold you a career opportunity which you bought into and led you to the very job you're doing now.

Clearly, selling ourselves along our career journeys to attain our aspirations doesn't have to mean we're sleazy snake-oil salespeople; not if we remain in tune with our moral compass.

Staying attuned to your inner compass through your voyage of career success is key. Whether you aspire to move up, sideways or even down, it'll always help you remember the vital importance of a cornerstone skill or precept: self-belief. Above all else, you must believe in yourself. You have what it takes to achieve what you want. Don't let anyone tell you different; not even yourself.

Favorable Winds for Your Career Ship

IN ANY PROFESSIONAL FIELD, OUR understanding and use of our technical knowledge, or tools of the trade, is akin to the familiarity and expertise a car mechanic builds up about, say, a hydraulic wrench or multimeter. It's a body of knowledge acquired from her training and subsequent years on the job. But you wouldn't keep taking your car to that car mechanic's garage if she had a lousy attitude and despicable behavior.

No customer would. (Unless, of course, circumstances made that impossible.)

Her knowledge and skills with technical tools like the wrench, the multimeter and being able to diagnose and fix car problems make her a "mechanic." But to ensure her garage business remains successful over the long term, the mechanic must also be able to interact with her customers and manage their concerns with reasonable levels of consideration and decency. She must have people smarts.

This same requirement for savoir faire with the "people" dimensions of work applies to us all, whatever professional field we work in and whatever career goals we're pursuing.

Just as the mechanic's technical proficiency makes her a mechanic, so too does our technical competency make us marketers or marketeers, accountants, florists, engineers, project managers, doctors, salespeople, scientists, and so on.

And just as the mechanic needs to be good with people to keep her business successful, so too do we need to be discerning with our colleagues, stakeholders and contacts in our networks to sustain our work success and ensure our careers prosper.

Being organizationally savvy is important. It's fundamentally about dexterity with people-related issues—having the right soft skills to navigate the organizational terrain with flair.

You can't possibly be a half-decent professional without the right technical skills. But to be effective and thrive, you must have highly developed soft skills. And second only to your ability to manage yourself, the most critical soft skills are your abilities to manage interactions with others.

It's those same interactions that provide bountiful opportunities to understand people and their scripts better, to shine your brand and help them on their own quests, and to sprinkle your gold dust.

Unless your career ambition is to become a hermit or a mad scientist locked away in your laboratory working in total isolation, you need the support, friendship or allyship of these people to get on at work and get ahead in your career.

Almost everyone works in an organization at some point in their career. And all organizations, at their core, are interconnections of people. Our ability as professionals to recognize this and tap into it is vital to our current work performance and long-term career success.

Our personal work style is an important factor here. But we may not fully appreciate the far-reaching ways it manifests itself. Some of these can be inconspicuous, yet directly and massively help or hinder our ability to thrive and flourish at work and in our careers. How we portray ourselves and our approach to the key human-to-human dynamics at play are central to this.

It's just plain ineffective to focus too much on the technical elements of our work and ignore or give inadequate attention to our relationships with colleagues and stakeholders. Because it's these same folks who'll join in your song to create a beautiful melody when you write the lyrics and start singing.

Quite simply, relationships matter.

Far more than many of us realize.

It's through your relationships with people at work and others in your career network that they get to see the brilliance of your star.

Unfortunately, I wasn't taught all this at university. And it took me a few years of my career and many frustrating experiences to eventually appreciate it. I came to learn that engaging people at work shrewdly, winning them over to our work agenda and sustaining positive relationships with them is a vital component of finding our groove and orchestrating fabulous success at work.

It's the very same success, coupled with other ingredients—like your passion, self-leadership, personal effectiveness and the power of your dreams—that propel you ever forwards to the career success you desire.

If you really want to get ahead, *proactively* managing your professional and workplace relationships must be an integral part of your modus operandi. You should be constantly sowing fertile seeds of trust and goodwill and nurturing a network of fans and allies, just as you're supporting others on their success journeys.

When you propagate amicability and good vibes like this, you're like an alchemist conjuring and conveying the chemistry of positive interpersonal connections—connections propagated through the ages, helping to keep humanity sane; connections which in your own work context can only benefit you and your career.

The affinity, rapport and kinship we generate and sustain in this way bring many merits related to our happiness and job satisfaction, and research studies show that this extends to our productivity and quality of work. You don't need to be a brain surgeon to recognize how this augments your flourishing and fulfillment.

Some people say it's karma: because you're diligent, helpful, likable, trustworthy and dependable with people (without expecting anything in return), you get all that good vibe back, through the conduit of your reputation.

And some say it's being a good gardener: planting and tending the seeds and outgrowths of the tree that will bear your ripe, juicy fruit—show the tree love and it gives you love back, in its own way. Likewise, show your colleagues, stakeholders and other connections love and you'll get it back in return, a love that acts as fertilizer for your career growth and success.

You'll find more in-depth insights and practical guidance to help you master this in my book *Sweet Stakeholder Love*.

In any case, always remember: relationships matter.

So try to devote a proportion of your work day or week—say, ten, fifteen, twenty percent of your time, or whatever feels right—to relationship-building. It's one of the savviest things to do for your career success.

Because if you can't get people on board with your work or career agenda, then all your technical knowledge is of limited value. Good people skills are like the favorable winds that sail your career ship, whatever the destination port you're aiming for.

Your ship is more likely to sail into port gracefully if it's got a captain who is adept in a well-rounded way—that's you.

You are the most important person to utilize your people skills on. And in some ways, that starts with your attitude; to yourself, your career dreams and your success.

Some people don't typically think of attitude as a skill. And we could indeed argue the semantics of it. Whatever the case, adopting and maintaining a positive attitude can be learned. It takes repeated practice and mental discipline. But it's a very worthwhile effort, and advisable too.

Knowledge and hard work are important, but your attitude is pivotal.

Having a positive attitude isn't simply about the widely touted notions of "positive thinking." It includes seemingly mundane things like knowing when and how to take action and when and how to be patient. Sometimes the best thing to "do" is to do nothing.

Likewise, knowing when and how to speak and when and how to be silent is also part of maintaining the right attitude. So too is knowing when to take time out or to rest. As is learning to trust yourself.

If you don't trust yourself, how can you possibly expect others to trust you with the career opportunities that'll form your success and shape your destiny?

Lack of self-trust impairs the flourish of the human spirit.

We must learn to trust ourselves steadfastly, undeterred by the doubts that may be niggling at our minds or the fears attacking our hearts.

Yet self-trust isn't about expecting yourself to take the perfect decisions or actions every time. Rather, you should trust yourself to find your groove. The more you try, the more you'll learn; and yes, some of that learning may entail making "mistakes"—the same mistakes a hatchling makes when it's trying to learn to stand on its limbs, to walk or to fly. That same hatchling eventually learns and succeeds. Its success comes because it continues to try; it continues to try because it trusts itself to ultimately achieve what it's trying to achieve. And so should you.

Trust that you have the capability to achieve your career dreams. Trust the knowledge and skills that you have. And trust your brain horsepower and your five senses. But trust your sixth sense too—your intuition, your inner silent knowledge, your gut instinct, or call it what you will.

Tuning into yourself and listening to the silent knowledge of your inner guru is one of the finest things to do to realize your dreams. Your inner guru is a phenomenal companion that can help you rock to a sweeter tempo. It's an aid that is relied upon by many of the most successful people in all walks of life, people who are wiser, more experienced and more accomplished than me; people who consciously adopt the attitude of listening to themselves.

If you cultivate the habit of tapping into your inner guru, it will bring tremendous value to your endeavors on your career voyage. And over time, you'll be astounded at how much wisdom lies dormant within you; wisdom which you awaken into an active and gainful state by habitually returning to hang out with the sage within you.

Hanging out with your inner guru is like having regular meetings with yourself. And a meeting with yourself is the most important meeting you'll ever attend.

Unlike many of the wasteful ones we often have at work, meetings with yourself are always fruitful—once you enforce the personal discipline to actually sit still and have the meeting, rather than procrastinate or find excuses not to.

The habit of regularly carving out time to scrutinize yourself and consider things properly, through the prism of life and learning, is so invaluable that many top performers in any field have made it integral to their lives. Some go away on periodic retreats or sojourns to impel the discipline, others *make the time* in their normal lives and keep it sacrosanct.

That's the salient bit: recognizing that these meetings with yourself are sacred—because you are important;

whether the meetings are held in your bedroom, the garden shed, by the river, in the forest, under the willow tree or at the kitchen table.

Spending time with your inner authentic self, in complete solitude without any distractions, is an opportunity to recalibrate yourself to your inner compass, to realign your everyday self with the special, unique gift you have inside, the spark in you that is your mojo. It's a time for refuge from the flurry and frenzy of everyday life, and any work difficulties or career challenges you may be grappling with. A time for reflection, rejuvenation, insights and guidance, which strengthens the connection to your best self. A time for complete self-honesty, without the hindrance of your ego, the "mask" you wear at work, the façade you present to the world or the self-delusion of the little white lies we all tell ourselves day in, day out.

We lie to ourselves about all sorts of things—including, why we're failing to ingrain the habits we know are good for us; why we cannot or might not achieve our dreams; why we're struggling to jettison the attitudes and patterns we know are hindering us from discovering our inner magic; why endless group chats and other forms of behavioral cocaine are essential to our existence; why we're not yet putting into practice the things we learned from that book, podcast or webinar which intuitively resonated with our spirit; …

It's all a load of baloney.

And we know it deep down inside.

Yet we keep deluding ourselves with these lies, which often impede our ability to reveal our best selves and harness our mojo. These delusions frequently seem inconsequential at the time we make them. But with the passage of time, they can accumulate and derail us from our path.

Little white lies, behavioral cocaine and other strands of personal ineffectiveness obscure the clarity of our dreams and cloud the brilliance of our potential, like clouds that shroud the brightness of the sun. They are unfavorable winds that can be insidious saboteurs of our career ship; they deliver their impact over the long term, when it may be too late to remedy their effects on our destiny.

Rather than indulging in such unproductiveness, it's so much better for our success and well-being to face up to our failings or shortcomings, and celebrate our strengths and triumphs. And that's part of the essence of meetings with yourself, the special moments to behold and ingest the truths of your heart; truths which bring meaning and purpose to your career voyage, the most auspicious winds to set your sails to.

If you intentionally schedule the time, and use it correctly, the practice of quiet rumination and tapping the sage wisdom of your inner guru will yield leaps in your growth, capabilities, judgment and success; it'll be a priceless boon for your career—when you form it into a habit.

If you don't cultivate the habit, you'll frequently end up reacting to outside events, circumstances or people, rather than responding with self-assurance. You could become an unwitting puppet to external factors pulling your strings. This isn't what you want, nor what you'd describe as sailing with favorable winds.

As your career ship sails through the many tides and seasons of your voyage, some pleasurable and some not, you'll experience circumstances of various sorts. It's the attitude you *choose* to adopt, especially toward the "negative" or "difficult" experiences, that will largely determine how your journey pans out—because how we perceive and respond to situations is often more important than the situations themselves. This is an essential aspect of the arsenal of soft skills we all need to triumph.

Remember this as you sit in the captain's chair navigating your career ship to the port named Success.

Nuggets for Your Success

***

People often think career success or on-the-job perfor-mance is purely dependent on having the right technical skills. Yet the prevalent evidence shows that the most effective and successful professionals tend to be those with highly developed soft skills—the crucial intrapersonal and interpersonal competencies that will help drive your career success.

***

***

Unfortunately, we don't often learn about honing our skills for success in conventional academic studies. And most people don't invest adequately in their career and personal development—they jump on the career treadmill and, really, leave their destiny in others' hands.

❖ That's one of the reasons only a small minority of the population in any field are winners.
❖ A significant proportion of people go to their graves without discovering and harnessing the best of their capabilities—they die with their music still inside them and that's sad.

Will *you* be a winner?

***

***

We all have the capacity to develop new skills or refine our capabilities. We just need to recognize the importance to our careers, and get whatever learning and help we need to unleash our potential. Doing this will be one of the best investments you'll make in your career success.

***

***

Oftentimes, developing new skills or honing your abilities is like forming new habits—practice or repetition and persistence are key; just like learning to ride a bicycle.

***

***

Self-care is an important skill for success. Learn to look after your physical, mental, emotional and spiritual health.

***

***

Get enough sleep.

Just that.

It sounds simple. Maybe even stupid, or obvious. And perhaps not what you expect to read or hear as advice for career success. Yet it's one of the keystones of personal excellence and credible success.

It's also highly underappreciated. Because we live in a world of hustle and bustle, where being busy is often perceived (sometimes subconsciously) as making progress or a sign of success. And some people wear the badge of sleeping so little with pride. We've fallen for the fallacy that busy, successful people need less shut-eye. Yet many of us are busy fools, busy doing nothing.

Adequate, good-quality sleep is a pillar of your career prosperity, as many scientific studies have shown. It profits your mental clarity, energy, focus, performance, creativity, memory, decision-making, … even your relationships—including with yourself. That's why most top performers in business and other fields value and prioritize their sleep; they sustain the habit of getting enough sleep.

So should you.

***

***

Know your values.
Value your happiness.
And always appreciate yourself.

***

***

Examples of other valuable soft skills include: action orientation; adaptability, e.g., to change or ambiguity; assertiveness; customer focus—including your own internal customers; emotional intelligence; goal-setting; initiative; leadership—especially of yourself; organizational savvy—knowing how to leverage organizational dynamics; perseverance; presentation—of information and yourself; professionalism; results orientation; self-belief; self-discipline; self-awareness, e.g., be aware of your strengths and development needs, and the consequences of what you think, say and do; self-motivation; time management (so-called; but you can't really "manage" time)—investing your time effectively.

***

***

"Many of us have to constantly keep our skills base relevant for today's workplace, and we also have to think about the skills that will be required for the future.

It's part of the life of being a professional. And it applies in most, if not all, fields—#engineering, #procurement, #marketing, #HR, #projectmanagement, #supplychain, …

It even applies to car mechanics, farmers and voodoo magicians. We've all got to keep our skills fresh.

Yet it's not just the pure 'technical' competencies of our particular field we must be adept at, but also any relevant technological innovations. And right now #technology is a huge and ever-growing element in almost every field.

Within this 'skills race,' it can be so easy to forget the vital importance of also nurturing our #softskills.

It's worth remembering that, whatever happens with the relentless march of technology, as long as there are humans in the workplace then soft skills will remain vital for *effective* human interactions AND self-leadership."

— Linkedin.com/in/SigiOsagie

***

***

Sometimes all you have to do is sit still, tune in and listen to your inner guru, the fount of the immeasurable capabilities within you.

You can't hear your inner guru if you're talking (verbally, with your mouth, or mentally, with your mind) all the time.

***

***

The meaning and purpose of your life and career is etched and embedded in your mojo. Yet it's not always easy for us to "see" this and grasp it—perhaps because it's expressed in a language beyond words in our internal universe; or because we're handicapped by our overreliance on logic and reason; or because we're hindered by our fixation with the outside world and our addiction to behavioral cocaine.

Yet the message and guidance are always there for us.

Hanging out with your inner guru habitually will ease the task of disinterring the message in your mojo, and give you direction to set the sails of your career ship to.

***

Sigi Osagie
@SigiOsagie

Sage words. The best
mentors can indeed change
the dynamics and trajectory
of your #work or #career
journey.

> "There's a lot to be said for either
> picking, or being lucky enough to
> land, the right mentor. The best ones
> can change your life."
>
> – Sir Alex Ferguson
> in *Leading*, with Sir Michael Moritz

***

"Does the #work you do, the organization you do it in, or the boss you work for bring out the best in you and make you feel truly fulfilled?

If not, you should ask yourself why.

And don't wait for things to change; change things yourself—'could be your perspectives, your thought processes, your attitude to the job, or maybe even changing jobs and moving to something that gets your juices flowing and helps you unleash your mojo.

Remember, your mojo won't come looking for you unless you go looking for it."

— Linkedin.com/in/SigiOsagie

***

Sigi Osagie   ■ ■ ■
Writer, Speaker, Business Adviser & Coach +
Mentor. Author, SWEET STAKEHOLDER
LOVE, and other books to up your game
4y · Edited

Cheryl Strayed's words below make a lot of
sense to me. They also make me ponder: how
can we be truly happy at #work if for most of
the time we're wearing a 'mask' in order to fit in,
rather than being our true selves?

The more you stay true to yourself, the more
you'll discover whether or not the work you're
doing, the boss you're working for and the
organization you work in are conducive to the
flourishing of your mojo.

Let your discovery guide how you steer your
#career ship. And never let anyone else sit in
the captain's chair of that ship — because it's
yours!

"True happiness isn't a life without
strife, but one where your inner
and outer self are as close as they
can be."

— Cheryl Strayed

in *The Sunday Times Magazine*, October 9, 2016

Sigi Osagie

Writer, Speaker, Business Adviser & Coach +
Mentor. Author, SWEET STAKEHOLDER
LOVE, and other books to up your game

4y

If the organization you #work for, or your direct
boss, does not appreciate your #talent and
contribution, then maybe you should be
somewhere else where your soul can sing its
song.

Or, maybe YOU need to appreciate yourself
more.

Appreciating yourself will help you recognise
the immeasurable capabilities within you. And,
maybe, then you won't let your boss or the
organization you work in stifle the flourishing of
the song in your soul.

***

If your self-belief is low, and holding you back from realizing your career dreams, one of the simplest things you can do is to start practicing selling yourself to yourself; a bit like you would do in a job application or interview.

For example, *regularly* and *persistently* remind yourself of your positive traits, your strengths and abilities, your experience, your past achievements and all the wonderful things you know about yourself—even if there are only three. Just start with that. Feed your psyche with this elevator pitch, just as you feed your body with food. And act accordingly.

*

Self-belief is not vanity.

Neither is it egotism, self-centeredness, being pompous or boastful, overestimating your abilities, or thinking you're flawlessly and supremely superfly.

And it isn't putting yourself down, doubting your potential, toxifying your spirit with negative self-talk, or acting and living your life based on limiting thoughts and perceptions.

It's an inner assuredness about yourself, a feeling and attitude of confidence without arrogance, like being comfortable in your own skin. Because you know who you are.

***

***

As you craft your career destiny, try not to rely exclusively or excessively on logic and rational reasoning or your five senses alone. What you perceive inside—your sixth sense, intuition, gut instinct, your inner silent knowledge or call it what you will—is a powerful aid that can help you unlock your potential.

Your inner guru often indicates valuable truths and guidance that your rational faculties can't detect or fathom.

Think how often you use this knowledge beyond reason almost every day without questioning. For instance, when you "just know, somehow" that something isn't quite right with your child. Or when you "can just tell" that your spouse or your close friend is unsettled or deeply unhappy even when their outward behavior is normal. Or when you sense that your mistress or gigolo is lying to you.

You're using this capacity in your private life already without trying to reason out *how* you know what you know. So why not leverage it in your work life as a navigational aid in sailing your career ship to the destination port named Success?

The more you hone your ability to use this aid, the more faithfully and significantly it will serve you.

***

***

"We are all 'experts' in something, in our own unique, individual way. So have faith in yourself—go ahead and strut your stuff. And don't let anyone stop you."
— @SigiOsagie

***

***

As you make progress on your career journey and become more and more successful, it's natural and pleasurable to bask in the glory of your specific victories or your general success. But never let your accomplishments or progress go to your head.

If you start thinking you're flawlessly and supremely superfly, you can lose your sense of who you truly are and become a vainglorious nitwit. This insidious risk manifests when our ego grows unhealthily larger than our gratitude and starts to submerge our spirit in self-conceit.

None of us is really that superfly. Any of us can be brought down by a simple cold or a broken heart. And the simple algae and the humble bee both contribute more to life than any of us do.

So remember to stay grounded—even as you sip the sweet nectar of success up there with the gods.

***

Unleash Your Mojo for Career Success

It's SAD BUT TRUE THAT many people leave their career growth at the mercy of their employers or bosses. People who take ownership of their career destiny are much more likely to attain success; because once you reach out for your mojo, it reaches out for you too.

You already have the abilities to do great things in your life and in your career, greater than the achievements you've made so far. Listen to your guru: yourself. Because that's where your mojo is—it's the best version of yourself that is already in you.

And that best self has a good sense of how to emerge; if you'll give it the chance and do your bit to aid its release.

Your mojo doesn't care whether you work in Marketing, IT, Finance, or the local convenience store.

It simply wants to be unleashed and manifested in your career success.

Unleashing your mojo starts with you and the fire of the human spirit in your belly.

Immeasurable capabilities abound in the human spirit, the same spirit that brought us the steam engine, penicillin and the internet, the same spirit embodied in all the great souls of renowned accomplishments through the history of time. That same spirit resides in you.

Look how far you've come, how many obstacles you've overcome, how many mountains you've climbed and conquered, to get to this point in your career. And you have the potential for greater successes.

Whatever your story, whatever your background, you have the capacity to achieve extraordinary things—because you were born with your mojo in you.

Your mojo is your personal gift, the gift of inner success which we're all born with. But you must unwrap that gift to manifest it in the outer world.

Unwrapping your gift is sweeter when the work you do as you build your career inspires you and rouses your spirit. An endeavor imbued with passion and enthusiasm will always be much more enjoyable.

Of course, things may not always go smoothly, or you may feel as if you're not progressing fast enough.

If so, you're not alone.

Many of us sometimes get buffeted by the winds of time, circumstances and things that don't quite work out as we would like. In the worst cases, we may become overwhelmed by seemingly indomitable forces like frustration, impatience, doubt, fatigue, worry, and even stress and fear. Or we may be feeling disheartened and dejected. Our psyches may start to imbibe some unspoken notion that our dreams are beyond our reach. And before we know it, we actually start acting as if that's indeed true.

But is it?

Just because sometimes things may not feel like they're progressing to plan doesn't mean that things aren't progressing at all. There are always two plans unfolding and spurring you toward your mojo: your plan, and a slicker, more intelligent version written by life. When both are congruent is when we feel the *flow* in our work.

But we're all so much in a hurry that we frequently miss the markers life lays down for us. We forget that, quite often in life, to make fast progress toward your goals you have to go slow and focus on the path. When you go slow, you see more. And the more you see, the more you'll realize that you may also need to be patient so the fruits of your effort can ripen for your eventual benefit.

Making progress isn't about making haste, but about finding your rhythm and letting the tempo of your flow guide you to success.

Remember, a pigeon seems to move slowly as it walks with its pigeon steps, yet when the time is "right" it takes flight and moves swiftly with its wings. When you're in flow, totally immersed in the zone, it feels like your spirit is brimming full of rapture, as it glides effortlessly in a rhapsody of all that is good in life; your progress will happen at the right pace, and your career success will seem almost seamless.

You'll only ever have a good chance of attaining this through your personal effectiveness—being effective in how you go about your work, your career development, and making the most of your critical resources, e.g., your time, your attention, your thoughts and imagination, and your money.

In some of my talks, I often share the tale of Vincent to simplify the meaning of personal effectiveness. In the days soon after the national lottery was first launched in the UK, Vincent had gone through a life-planning exercise in which he decided that what he wanted in life was to enjoy a millionaire lifestyle, with all the trappings that would bring.

Having clarified his goal, he decided that his route-path to achieve it would be to win the lottery. So, come Saturday evening, shortly before the lottery draw program aired on TV, Vincent was up in his bedroom, on his knees, saying a prayer, "Please God, please God, let me win the lottery."

The lottery draw TV program came on, the presenters read out the winning lottery numbers and Vincent didn't win.

The following Saturday, he was up in his bedroom again, on his knees repeating his prayer, "Please God, please God, let me win the lottery. I promise to take my wife shopping, to be nicer to my kids, to give some of the money to charity …"

The lottery draw program came on TV shortly after, the winning numbers were read out, and yet again Vincent didn't win the lottery.

But Vincent had one of the important traits we all need for success: perseverance. So come the next Saturday, there he was again on his knees in his bedroom, "Please God, please God, let me …" Before he got any further in his prayer he suddenly heard a great, booming voice coming from nowhere and everywhere: "Come on man, will you stop hassling me; at least meet me halfway and buy a ticket!"

Just as you can't win the lottery without buying a ticket, you can't achieve career success without taking the right actions to achieve that success.

Some of us are often hampered in our personal effectiveness by perceived or self-created barriers, such as:

❖ Excuses and little white lies. "The cat jumped over the wall and that stopped me from spending an hour on reviewing my career goals yesterday." Or, "The monkey fell off the tree ..."

❖ Pleasure. Giving priority to things that give us pleasure over things that take us toward our goals.

❖ Peer group. If you spend most of your time with successful people, those who have achieved or are striving to achieve the success, traits or results you desire, it impacts your subconscious positively. Likewise, if you spend most of your time with people with little or no personal effectiveness, it also impacts you.

  • Think about this, which do you think is more beneficial: spending your time with a group of successful people regularly or with a bunch of hoodlums?

❖ Procrastination. "Let me just make a cup of tea first, then I'll settle down and work on my CV." Or, "I'll do it tomorrow."

❖ Busyness. Quite often we try to disguise our avoidance by being very busy doing things that may be interesting but don't contribute toward the attainment of our goals.

❖ Environments. Allowing ourselves to become puppets of the environments we're in, by doing what everyone else does or what others expect of us; and getting caught up in what's happening *out there* (the myriad dramas and distractions) and missing the broadcast from *in here* (our own authentic inner compass).

❖ Fear. Fear of failure; fear of not being loved; fear of dreaming; fear of … this and that. When you live life from fear, your life is always stunted. To paraphrase Spencer Johnson, the fear you allow to grow in your mind is almost always worse than the reality.

As well as staying aware of these factors, one of the simplest ways to assess your personal effectiveness is to examine how you spend your time and money, two currencies we all understand.

If career success is truly important to you but you spend little or no time on your career development or personal growth, yet you always watch your favorite TV program or you always find time for the cinema or five-a-side soccer every week, … Hmmm … Some people spend more money on their satellite TV subscription, gym membership or clothes shopping each year than they do on their career development.

Would you class this as being effective?

Personal effectiveness means doing the right things to get what you want; focusing those critical resources on the things that are most important to get you where you want to be in your career.

But where do you want to be?

Do you know what you really want for and from your career?

Are your aspirations tainted by outside influences and fads, or shaped by the true inner dreams and desires in the depths of your heart?

What do you genuinely desire—what are your career goals?

Your goals are the North Star of your career journey. They give you focus on your aspirations, your dreams and the career destiny you desire; whether it's to get a promotion in 2 years, to become a director in 1 year, to become CEO in 5 years or to set up your own business in 9 months.

Having clarity of your goals, the bona fide yearnings of your spirit—in your mind or in writing—will always move you closer to the diamond version of yourself and help you shape your destiny with greater success.

But having a goal without a route-map or game plan to achieve it is somewhat feeble. Planning is how you get from point A to point B. Or how to achieve "X" outcome or result, whether it's the New Kalamazoo Highway construction project or your loft-extension project. It's the same with your career.

Think of your career plan as a rough draft of your route-map to success. It shouldn't be like a divine blueprint set in tablets of stone, because you don't have one hundred percent forward visibility or certainty of all the events and circumstances of your career journey. So stay flexible to recognize when life is giving you a better set of opportunities.

Sometimes such hidden opportunities can appear on your path looking like obstacles, difficulties or challenges. Or they may be past endeavors that you view as failures, or experiences that felt like suffering.

Once you start making a committed effort to up your game and attain your success, you'll start learning some remarkable things from your experiences. You'll learn, for example, that growth often feels like suffering, and that life sometimes gives you what you need to achieve your goals rather than what you think you want—those challenges and failures are great examples.

Challenges usually entail stretching yourself and learning something new, which is how we grow. And quite often, our greatest failures are our best teachers, just as the deepest sufferings may hold the greatest insights and learning for us; if we reflect on the lessons gleaned from the experience.

Many of us commonly miss the concomitant lessons, as the challenges hoodwink us into forgetting that we remain conquerors capable of outstanding conquests.

Typically, it's because we give so much more of our attention to the problem or impediment. Our fixation with a challenge or its origins can have the insidious effect of reinforcing and amplifying the challenge, feeding it energy through our attention, and making it so gargantuan and powerful that we begin to doubt our ability to overcome it. Our doubt starts to chip away at our self-belief. And often, this is all happening below the surface.

It happens to all of us from time to time, whether we're battling challenges in life or at work. And it can be particularly acute when we feel we've made "mistakes" or "wrong" decisions, or when we face a devil of a challenge and we're quaking in our boots.

Yet, as I've experienced and witnessed repeatedly, the very same challenges that make us forget who we truly are can also expose the awesome capabilities within each and every one of us; depending on how *we choose* to respond to the experience.

We can choose to recognize that the growth of our wisdom is in experiencing the challenge or the apparent wrongness of our decision or action.

And we can choose to surrender to the lessons the experience proffers.

Those lessons might include gaining the wisdom that the human spirit has unparalleled strength and fortitude within it. Even in the face of untold suffering and seemingly insurmountable barriers, we have something inside us that is so strong and wise, something resilient that is always there for us to tap into, a force or power that resides within *every one* of us and can help us overcome the toughest challenges or most formidable impediments. But to leverage this inborn power, we've got to devote time and attention to "looking inside" where the power resides, rather than becoming fixated with the outside world where the challenge originates—looking outside, at the world around you, can teach you a lot; looking inside, at the world inside you, can teach you even more.

That special place inside you is the same receptacle that holds the precious lessons you accumulate from your various experiences, lessons you draw upon repeatedly as you advance your career journey.

So, adversities like failures, challenges and sufferings frequently offer bountiful rewards in ways we may not see at the time. Because they're typically disguised by the wrapping paper they come in. You should bear this in mind whenever you review your progress against your plan—which you'll no doubt do periodically and earnestly, at least once a year.

When you have your scheduled career-plan reviews, you mustn't be despondent about anything, nor beat yourself up about things that haven't gone as you'd like. That's just a pointless waste of energy.

If you know in your heart of hearts that you've been lazy or irresponsible with your career growth and personal development, then acknowledge this with total self-honesty. And perhaps deal with yourself as you'd deal with a member of your staff who is holding the team back by their unsatisfactory performance (maybe be a bit tougher).

If you know you're giving your all and doing your best in striving to realize your career dreams, then you can't ask more of yourself. Your efforts and dedication will be rewarded; continue to give the endeavor your best and you'll see your best get better.

There's a great deal of satisfaction that flows to your psyche when you know you're doing your best, which is helpful to your mojo, and is recognized by life. And that satisfaction is greatly amplified when your best endeavors start to bear fruit.

Career-plan reviews are great times to remind yourself of the potential within you. Life will always give you more opportunities to discover and harness that potential. Be confident in yourself and seize them; because life is confident in you.

That confidence should be substantiated by your decision to choose yourself and your resolve to align yourself to your career dreams—especially through your everyday actions; because ultimately, action is what counts.

Many people fantasize about their dream job or career without ever taking real, tangible actions to realize their dream. Some read loads of books or watch countless on-line webinars, videos and TED talks without really taking action either. Others engage coaches or mentors, sub-scribe to numerous podcasts or attend various seminars, workshops and training courses but still never really get going. And some go as far as planning but don't actually act on their plan.

Choosing yourself means betting on yourself. And aligning yourself means taking real, intentional actions to win that bet, i.e., actually doing something, taking concrete steps, physically laying down the stones or bricks to build your career castle—*that* is real, tangible action.

Books, videos, courses or coaches may be useful, but in themselves will not construct your castle.

For instance, looking back now, I can see that when I was dreaming of having a corporate career rather than mopping floors and cleaning toilets for a living, as well as attending a university course to get the requisite qualifi-cation, I also had to sit my butt down and physically pen many application letters to sell myself to the companies I wanted to work for. Similarly, when I aspired to become an independent consultant, as well as finding out how from various sources and drawing up my game plan, at some point I also had to pick up the phone and start speaking to prospective clients I thought I could help with my expertise, and keep at it while tweaking my approach until I secured my first assignment. And when I first started dreaming of my writing desk atop my Spanish castle, as well as learning how to become a successful writer from books, seminars and a writing coach, I physically had to open my laptop every day to actually write; because a writer writes—500 words, 1,000 words, 2,000 or whatever, consistently; words that appear on screen or on paper as the building blocks of the writer's career castle, words which you're now hopefully benefiting from as you read them here, and you would never have gained the benefit if I didn't pragmatically take action and truly get started as a writer.

So, take consistent action to achieve what you want.

Don't be a dabbler with your career success; dabbling will get you nowhere—if you dabble with success, success might also dabble with you.

Don't do things only when you feel like it or feel motivated; waiting for motivation will do you no favors—motivation follows action.

Don't wait to be chosen by others or wait for things to happen; make them happen. That's the gift of your mojo—you have the ability to make things happen.

Start now, today—do something concrete and specific that will aid you in unleashing your mojo and achieving the career success you desire.

Taking action means taking responsibility, which you must. You are the CEO of "My Career Inc." So don't wait for your boss or your employer to develop your career; there's only one person who can unleash your mojo—guess who that is!

Nuggets for Your Success

***

Most of us are pulled in different directions, from pillar to post, in everyday life—social engagements, sports activities, hobbies, household chores, catching our favorite TV shows, rendezvous with lovers and mistresses, etc. We end up ignoring the one thing that pays for most of the other things: our careers.

***

***

Focusing on effectiveness forces us to question the actions we are taking in the present, today, and how they relate to the career goals we are targeting.

***

***

Some of the building blocks of personal effectiveness can be distilled into examining what we spend our time on; what we focus our thoughts on; what we do, and how we act or behave. So ask yourself these questions as regards your work success and career development:

❖ What do I actually spend my time on?
❖ How much of that time is spent on thinking, and how much on doing?
❖ Do I spend the bulk of my time on things that are truly important rather than things that are merely urgent?
❖ What do I consciously focus my thoughts on, or what thoughts do I allow to occupy my mind?
❖ What do I actually do—what actions do I take?

***

***

If you waste your time and brain horsepower ineffec-
tively, rather than focusing on the important things that
will move you toward your career aspirations, then you
are damaging your personal effectiveness and negating
your mojo.

***

***

Give your attention (time, effort, money, etc.) to the things that are truly important to take you toward your career goals. And continuously invest in your growth and development.

***

***

Outlining your career goals, or defining them in detail, demands sound thinking, balancing the requirement to keep learning and growing, your short- to medium-term desires, and your long-term aspirations.

***

***

In setting your goals and planning your route-map:

❖ Try to make your career goals aligned with your personal values and your happiness.

❖ Think about how you're going to achieve your goals—the stepping stones, opportunities, experiences or support you may need.

❖ You may need to stretch yourself. Do something (e.g., a task, a role, a job move, a new habit) that's outside your comfort zone but will aid your progress toward your ultimate career goals, perhaps by expanding your horizons.

• When we do things from our comfort zone, we're not growing.

• Stretch is good. When we stretch, we grow. It's the same way you build muscle—by pushing beyond what you think you're capable of. (But don't over-stretch and create stress.)

❖ You should have a degree of congruence between the things you aim for in the short term and what you really want in the long term. It may be wiser to start with the latter and work backwards.

❖ Don't overcomplicate things. Otherwise you'll never get started or achieve very much.

❖ Remember, career development is not always about climbing up the ladder. It's more about the experiences you need to get you where you want to go. Identify those opportunities and seize them boldly.

***

***

Practice and develop the habit of taking intentional action. E.g., do something focused and specific now, today, that will take you toward your career goals; or write down the critical actions you will take each day, week or month, *and follow through* by doing those things—use your personal discipline to make yourself do what you committed to do.

***

***

It's very helpful to maintain a positive mindset and consistently think empowering thoughts about your future, even when things may seem difficult or challenging.

It takes a determined mindset to excel, and concerted and persistent efforts at doing the right things.

It may not be easy, but it's only ever as difficult as riding a bicycle was before you learned to ride one.

***

***

Creating time to regularly sit down and reflect on your personal effectiveness, your ongoing development and your career goals is a great habit to cultivate.

***

***

Monitor your progress on your career path, and adjust your plans and actions if necessary. "Walk to the balcony"—step away from things—frequently for candid self-assessment.

***

***

Try to assess career opportunities and the choices or decisions you make against your career goals or long-term aspirations.

***

***

You can usually tell someone's got their mojo from their vibe and how they comport themselves, the way they roll. They tend to be reasonably comfortable in their own skin. Their personal brand is credible; their integrity is sound; and their personal effectiveness stands out—especially in their ability to deliver results and maintain good inter-personal relationships at work, while continually moving themselves forwards on their career path.

Have you got yours?

***

Sigi Osagie
Writer, Speaker, Business Adviser & Coach +
Mentor. Author, SWEET STAKEHOLDER
LOVE, and other books to up your game
3y · Edited

Your mojo doesn't care whether you work in
#Marketing, HR, #Finance, #Procurement,
R&D, Sales, IT or the local convenience store. It
simply wants to be unleashed and manifested in
your success.

Don't leave your career growth at the mercy of
your employer, your boss or chance.

People who take ownership of their #career
destiny are much more likely to attain success
— because once you reach out for your mojo, it
reaches out for you too.

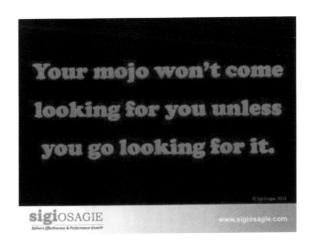

***

"January is the time of the year when many of us set ourselves all sorts of goals in our personal and professional lives—our New Year resolutions; which are really new mountains to climb and conquer.

Our resolutions may be to secure a new job, get a promotion, change career, get a new mistress or gigolo, … or to invest more in ourselves to bring out our best selves and unleash the immeasurable capabilities of the human spirit within us.

But will we actually achieve our goals or desires—will we climb that mountain and conquer it?

It all depends … on whether or not YOU are a mountain climber and you're prepared to 'build muscle.'"

— Linkedin.com/in/SigiOsagie

***

***

"Stress and fear are two of the worst adversaries that can impede your #careersuccess.

Stretch yourself so you can grow, but don't overstretch and create stress.

And feel the fear because fear is natural, but don't act from fear so you don't stunt your #careergrowth."

— @SigiOsagie

***

***

Dreaming big is great and worthwhile. Remembering that dreams don't build castles and castles don't build themselves is wise. And channeling your energies into building your career castle is shrewd.

But pursuing your goals shouldn't take over your life and stop you from enjoying the now.

So savor what you have already—the material and non-material; be thankful for your blessings and enjoy life as it is where you are here and now.

***

***

"Give your full attention to whatever you're doing right
now, even if it's just breathing."
— @SigiOsagie

***

***

Effectiveness is central to success in any realm of life.

It's about taking the right actions to achieve the outcomes you want.

You can't win the lottery without buying a lottery ticket.

Yet in the lottery of career success, the prize always exceeds the price; because luck isn't an accident for those who buy a ticket.

And you're one of them—if you think so, if you believe so, if you act so.

***

The Most Important Book
You Should Read

His name was Shaka, and he wore the name with pride.

He knew his parents had chosen that name because they hoped the gods would bless him with the greatness of Shaka kaSenzangakhona, the famous Zulu king and conqueror.

Indeed, for most of his own life he had felt that greatness with a silent inner knowing, without ever letting his ego trick him into believing he was greater than any other human. He always remembered the wisdom of the elders: "Everyone has greatness within them. Each one of us just has to search for it within our souls, and when we find it we must put it to good use."

He had used those sage words as one of his guiding principles in life, and the tenet had served him well.

But he also knew it wasn't always easy in practice, with all the challenges everyday life threw at him. Sometimes it felt as if life itself was testing him and he was often having to prove the greatness he knew he was blessed with.

He was going through one of those tests right now as he sought to make big strides in his vocation and realize his dreams of great success. And not for the first time, his search and his grapples with the challenge had led him to a conversation with his mentor.

As he sat in the seafront café in Santa Cruz, taking occasional sips of his warm *barraquito* and idly watching the world go by, he recalled what his mentor had said to him in that last conversation:

"The most important book you should read is one titled *Myself*.

It was published on the date you were born, by a project team with inconceivable powers, made up of God, Allah, Big Bang, Brahman, Yahweh, Nature, Buddha, Gaia, Shàng Dì, Olodumare, Waheguru, Ahura Mazda and a few other team members, with a little bit of help from your mother and father.

The book isn't available on Amazon, Barnes & Noble, Apple Books Store, Kobo or other book outlets. You don't need to buy it, as you already have it.

It has many chapters—the same number of chapters as the number of years in your life. And a new chapter is added every year you celebrate your birthday.

Every successful person I know of has read this book.

The book is a bestseller and has received critical acclaim from many quarters. It contains untold learning and wisdom that will help you achieve brilliant success—as soon as you start reading it.

One of the most outstanding things about this book is that you get to choose the ending—you get to write the rest of it as soon as you start reading it. That's awesome! Of course, if you feel it's too much responsibility, then you don't have to; you can always let other people write the ending and you just read the book and see how it ends.

If you don't like reading books, then watch the most important movie you should watch: it's also titled *Myself.*

It's based on the book of the same title, and was released on the same day as the book. It's a blockbuster, but is not available on YouTube, Netflix, Disney+ or other media channels. I suspect you already know where to find it.

Every successful person I know of has watched this movie.

The movie has also been highly praised by many. And just like the book, it's packed with insightful scenes and shrewd teachings that'll help you achieve dazzling success—as soon as you start watching it.

Amazingly, you get to choose how the movie ends! You become the director of the movie as soon as you start watching it. But you don't have to; if you feel it's too much responsibility.

And if you don't like watching movies or reading books, then listen to the most important song you should hear: it's also titled *Myself*.

It's the soundtrack to the movie, and was also released on the same day as the movie and the book. It's not available on iTunes Store, SoundCloud, Spotify or other music outlets. But I have a really strong sense that you know exactly where to find it.

Every successful person I know of has listened to this song.

The song is a chart-topper. And just like the movie and the book, it has been greatly lauded and is packed with inspiring lyrics and stirring melodies that will help you achieve magnificent success—as soon as you start listening to it.

And you get to decide how the song ends; although that isn't compulsory, not if you really don't want to become the record producer.

Even better than each of the three options is the multimedia package—try all three together: the book, the movie and the song. You'll be astounded by what you will discover. And your discovery will propel you in remarkable ways to the success you desire.

I don't know if you'll choose the multimedia pack, or just the book, the movie or the song. But in any case, please join me in a toast—let's drink to your brilliant success!"

Shaka smiled to himself. He raised his glass of *barraquito* with his absent mentor, in a silent toast to what he knew was coming. For him. And for you.

Nuggets for Your Success

***

Desire. Courage. Trust. Self-belief. Confidence. Action. Faith. Determination. Patience. Flexibility. Rest. Habits. Perseverance. Humor. Laughter. Self-discipline. Humility. Inner Wisdom. Victory.

***

***

Celebrate your successes, no matter how small they may seem. Tell yourself, "Well done, Me!" whenever you hit your stride or accomplish something. It's very good for your mojo.

***

***

As you climb the ladder of career success, make sure it's
leaning against the right wall.

***

Sigi Osagie
@SigiOsagie

"You should never be so preoccupied with what's happening 'out there' that you ignore what's happening 'in here'.

Your career success and overall wellbeing is determined more by what's inside than what's outside."

"Looking outside, at the world around you, can teach you a lot.

Looking inside, at the world inside you, can teach you even more."

© Sigi Osagie, 2017

sigiOSAGIE
Delivers Effectiveness & Performance Growth

www.sigiosagie.com

***

"You should never give up on your dreams—your
dreams never give up on you."
— @SigiOsagie

***

***

Your career success already exists—in the world of your dreams and imagination, from which the seeds of "reality" emanate. It's simply waiting patiently for you to actualize it in this physical world.

Every time you take a step toward it, it responds by taking two steps toward you; because it wants to manifest and embrace you just as much as you want to grasp it.

So go ahead and do so.

Don't doubt yourself.

Don't question your potential.

Don't let anyone or anything quench the fire in your belly or starve your spirit.

JUST GET GOING!

And keep nourishing yourself with soul food for your career success.

***

Thank You!

Dear reader, thank you for spending some of your most valuable assets—your money, your time and your attention—on this book. I hope it inspires and guides you to leverage the immeasurable capabilities within you, so you achieve the career success you desire.

If you enjoyed the book and found it useful, I'd love to hear your feedback: do post a positive review on all your preferred social media platforms and your bookseller's website; I'd appreciate that. Thank you.

I wish you an avalanche of blessings and triumphs on your career adventure. May the best days of your past be the worst days of your future.

*

"Monkey go London, monkey come back, monkey na still monkey; and e know say e be monkey."
— Mama Agbassa (Dorcas Abobo)

*

Notes

Most of the contents in this book are my ideas, principles and guidance on career success and workplace effectiveness, drawing on my own first-hand experiences and accumulated learning. I've shared some of this information previously, e.g., in some of my talks, media appearances and articles—I have adapted these earlier works for use here, noting below the publications or forums in which they first appeared. I have also indirectly drawn on other sources, as identified below.

1. Alter, Adam, "How Work Emails Affect Productivity" [Video], as displayed in Business Insider (@BusinessInsider), "Chances are, you won't

be as productive [...]" [Tweet], *https://twitter.com/ BusinessInsider*, July 30, 2018.

2. Andersson, Hilary, BBC Panorama, "Social Media Apps Are 'Deliberately' Addictive to Users," *www. bbc.co.uk*, July 4, 2018.

3. Bariso, Justin, "It Took Apple Executive Angela Ahrendts 1 Sentence to Drop the Best Career Advice You'll Hear Today," *www.inc.com*, January 17, 2018.

4. Berg, Yehuda, "The Kabbalists say [...]" [Wallet card], The Kabbalah Centre, London, UK, provided 2011.

5. Covey, Stephen R., *The 7 Habits of Highly Effective People*, Simon & Schuster, 2004.

6. Daisley, Bruce, "How Laughter Makes You a Better Worker," *www.bbc.com*, April 4, 2018.

7. Dyer, Wayne W., *10 Secrets for Success and Inner Peace*, Hay House, 2006.

8. Ferguson, Alex with Moritz, Michael, *Leading*, Hodder & Stoughton, 2015.

9. Gallo, Carmine, "Five Habits of the World's Most Creative Leaders," *www.forbes.com*, October 30, 2022.

10. Handy, Charles, *The Hungry Spirit*, Arrow Books, 1998.

11. Hill, Terry, *Manufacturing Strategy: The Strategic Management of the Manufacturing Function*, Second Edition, Macmillan, 1993.

12. Hughes, Tim (@Timothy_Hughes), "We are all born the same […]" [Tweet], *https://twitter.com/Timothy_Hughes*, April 30, 2015.

13. James, Oliver, *They F*** You Up: How to Survive Family Life*, Bloomsbury, 2003.

14. Johnson, Spencer, *Who Moved My Cheese?*, Vermilion, 1999.

15. Maber, Sarah, "A Life in the Day: Cheryl Strayed, Author," *The Sunday Times* (Magazine supplement), October 9, 2016.

16. Mullins, Laurie J., *Management and Organisational Behaviour*, Fourth Edition, Pitman Publishing, 1996.

17. Osagie, Sigi, "Boost Your Mojo, But Find It First! Strategies for Managing Your Growth and Development," motivational speeches at various branches of The Chartered Institute of Procurement & Supply (CIPS), UK, 2010–2011.

18. Osagie, Sigi, *Sweet Stakeholder Love*, EPG Solutions Limited, 2021.

19. Osagie, Sigi, "Unleash Your Mojo for Procurement Career Success," webinar for MarketSqr Procurement Africa e-Conference, May 2015.

20. Osagie, Sigi, various articles, feature contributions and social media posts, previously published on LinkedIn, Twitter, Facebook, *www.sigiosagie.com*, *www.epgsolutions.co.uk* and several other media outlets, 2006–2022.

21. Pechacek, Amy (@pechacek_amy), "The difference between success and failure is […]" [Tweet], *https://twitter.com/pechacek_amy*, July 20, 2022.

22. Welch, Jack and Suzy, "How I Hire: The Must-Haves, the Definitely-Should-Haves and the Game-Changer," *www.linkedin.com/pulse*, September 23, 2013.

Acknowledgments

THE KABBALISTS SAY THAT WHATEVER you imagine will come true. I don't know if my parents ever imagined that I'd become a writer (I did!), but here I am writing these words. And I'm here, able to do this, because of the start they gave me in life. So I thank them both—for their love and care, the upbringing they gave me, the values they instilled in me ... for everything: they provided the bedrock upon which to build my career success.

I'd also like to thank all the wise souls I've learned from on my career journey, especially the mentors who were instrumental to my growth and success at key stages: Hugh Humphrey, Ray Packe and Malcolm Hewitt; and express my gratitude to my readers, speaking audiences, clients and social media followers—their patronage and support is irreplaceable sustenance for my success.

Special thanks to the wonderful Dr. Noma Chinyere Osagie, my beta reader for the first edition of this book, and to my fabulous publishing team for their impeccable work: Karen "Elohor" Morton, Tanja "Alafia" Prokop, Graciela Aničić and Nigel D'Auvergne—may your blessings be more and nothing but happiness come through your door.

I'm immensely grateful to Preshe, the Gypsy Witch Earth Mother, for her unwavering encouragement, support and love—I appreciate you.

Finally, I give thanks to Love for all my blessings.

About the Author

SIGI OSAGIE HELPS ORGANIZATIONS AND individuals boost their workplace effectiveness to achieve their business and career goals.

He has extensive leadership experience across several sectors and continents, and previously held senior executive and board roles with a variety of blue-chip corporations and SMEs. His groundbreaking research on Management Effectiveness and Organizational Performance for his MBA informs much of his work.

Sigi arrived in the UK as a near barefoot and penniless immigrant; just fourteen years later he was a global director in a FTSE 250 multinational.

Today, he draws on insights from his atypical life journey and career success to inform and inspire others, through his work as a writer, speaker, business adviser and coach + mentor. His unique insights on the human spirit, the world of work and the adventure of life consistently imbue readers and audiences with wisdom and courage to reach beyond their perceived capabilities and achieve transformational success.

For more information or to contact Sigi, please visit www.sigiosagie.com.

———————

Stay in touch for more valuable content, insights and latest news via:

- ❖ Twitter: @SigiOsagie
- ❖ LinkedIn: https://uk.linkedin.com/in/sigiosagie
- ❖ Facebook: https://www.facebook.com/sigiosagie

*

"You are not a drop in the ocean, you are the entire ocean in a drop."
— Rumi

*

Index

Printed in Great Britain
by Amazon

16869122R00135